LITERATURE MADE EASY

WILLIAM SHAKESPEARE'S

the

MERCHANT

of VENICE

BARRON'S

First edition for the United States and Canada published by Barron's
Educational Series, Inc., 1999

First published in the United Kingdom by Hodder & Stoughton Ltd.
under the title: *Teach Yourself Literature Guides: A Guide to The
Merchant of Venice*

Cover photograph © Photo Stage/Donald Cooper
Mind Maps: David Orr
Illustrations: Karen Donnelly

American text edited by Elizabeth Schmid

All inquiries should be addressed to:
Barron's Educational Series, Inc.
250 Wireless Boulevard
Hauppauge, New York 11788
http://www.barronseduc.com

International Standard Book No. 0-7641-0826-3

Library of Congress Catalog Card No. 98-74652

Printed in the United States of America
9 8 7 6 5 4 3 2 1

CONTENTS

Important Note to Students About Line References
Line references are to The New Folger Library edition of Shakespeare's *The Merchant of Venice*. If you have another edition, the line numbers may vary slightly from those provided in this book, although the act and scene numbers should be the same. The line number references from the New Folger edition have been provided to help direct you to specific parts of the play, but often will not be an exact match for line numbers in other editions.

HOW TO STUDY

There are five important things you must know about your brain and memory to revolutionize the way you study:

- ◆ how your memory ("recall") works *while* you are learning
- ◆ how your memory works *after* you have finished learning
- ◆ how to use Mind Maps – a special technique for helping you with all aspects of your studies
- ◆ how to prepare for tests and exams.

Recall during learning
— THE NEED FOR BREAKS

When you are studying, your memory can concentrate, understand, and remember well for between 20 and 45 minutes at a time; then it needs a break. If you carry on for longer than this without a break your memory starts to break down. If you study for hours nonstop, you will remember only a small fraction of what you have been trying to learn, and you will have wasted hours of valuable time.

So, ideally, *study for less than an hour*, then take a five- to ten-minute break. During the break listen to music, go for a walk, do some exercise, or just daydream. (Daydreaming is a necessary brain-power booster – geniuses do it regularly.) During the break your brain will be sorting out what it has been learning, and you will go back to your books with the new information safely stored and organized in your memory banks. We recommend breaks at regular intervals as you work through this book. Make sure you take them!

Recall after learning
— THE WAVES OF YOUR MEMORY

What do you think begins to happen to your
memory right after you have finished learning something? Does it
immediately start forgetting? No! Your brain actually *increases* its
power and continues remembering. For a short time after your study
session, your brain integrates the information, making a more
complete picture of everything it has just learned. Only then does
the rapid decline in memory begin, and as much as 80 percent of
what you have learned can be forgotten in a day.

However, if you catch the top of the wave of your memory, and
briefly review (look back over) what you have been studying at the
right time, the memory is imprinted far more strongly, and stays at
the crest of the wave for a much longer time. To maximize your
brain's power to remember, take a few minutes at the end of a day
and use a Mind Map to review what you have learned. Then review
it at the end of a week, again at the end of a month, and finally a
week before your test or exam. That way you'll ride your memory
wave all the way there – and beyond!

The Mind Map ®
— A PICTURE OF THE WAY YOU THINK

Do you like taking notes? More important, do you like having to go
back over and learn them before tests or exams? Most students I
know certainly do not! And how do you take your notes? Most
people take notes on lined paper, using blue or black ink. The result,
visually, is boring. And what does *your* brain do when it is bored? It
turns off, tunes out, and goes to sleep! Add a dash of color, rhythm,
imagination, and the whole note-taking process becomes much
more fun, uses more of *your* brain's abilities, and improves your
recall and understanding.

Generally, your Mind Map is highly personal and need not be
understandable to any other person. It mirrors *your* brain. Its purpose
is to build up your "memory muscle" by creating images that will
help you recall instantly the most important points about the
characters and plot sequences in a work of fiction you are studying.

You will find Mind Maps throughout this book. Study them, add some color, personalize them, and then try drawing your own – you'll remember them far better. Stick them in your files and on your walls for a quick-and-easy review of the topic.

HOW TO DRAW A MIND MAP

1 First of all, briefly examine the Mind Maps and Mini Mind Maps used in this book. What are the common characteristics? All of them use small pictures or symbols, with words branching out from the illustration.

2 Decide which idea or character in the book you want to illustrate and draw a picture, starting in the middle of the page so that you have plenty of room to branch out. Remember that no one expects a young Rembrandt or Picasso here; artistic ability is not as important as creating an image you (and you alone) will remember. A round smiling (or sad) face might work as well in your memory as a finished portrait. Use marking pens of different colors to make your Mind Map as vivid and memorable as possible.

3 As your thoughts flow freely, add descriptive words and other ideas on the colored branching lines that connect to the central image. Print clearly, using one word per line if possible.

4 Further refine your thinking by adding smaller branching lines, containing less important facts and ideas, to the main points.

5 Presto! You have a personal outline of your thoughts about the character and plot. It's not a stiff formal outline, but a colorful image that will stick in your mind, it is hoped, throughout classroom discussions and final exams.

HOW TO READ A MIND MAP

1 Begin in the center, the focus of your topic.

2 The words/images attached to the center are like chapter headings; read them next.

3 Always read out from the center, in every direction (even on the left-hand side, where you will have to read from right to left, instead of the usual left to right).

USING MIND MAPS

Mind Maps are a versatile tool; use them for taking notes in class or from books, for solving problems, for brainstorming with friends, and for reviewing and working for tests or exams – their uses are endless! You will find them invaluable for planning essays for coursework and exams. Number your main branches in the order in which you want to use them and off you go – the main headings for your essay are done and all your ideas are logically organized!

Preparing for tests and exams

◆ Review your work systematically. Study hard at the start of your course, not the end, and avoid "exam panic."
◆ Use Mind Maps throughout your course, and build a Master Mind Map for each subject – a giant Mind Map that summarizes everything you know about the subject.
◆ Use memory techniques such as mnemonics (verses or systems for remembering things like dates and events).
◆ Get together with one or two friends to study, compare Mind Maps, and discuss topics.

AND FINALLY...

Have *fun* while you learn – it has been shown that students who make their studies enjoyable understand and remember everything better and get the highest grades. I wish you and your brain every success!

(Tony Buzan)

HOW TO USE THIS GUIDE

The guide assumes that you have already read *The Merchant of Venice*, although you could read Background and The Story of *The Merchant of Venice* before reading the play. It is best to use the guide alongside the text. You could read the Who's Who? and Themes sections without referring to the play, but you will get more out of these sections if you do refer to the play to check points made in these sections for yourself, and especially when thinking about the questions designed to test your recall and help you to think about the play.

The Commentary section can be used in a number of ways. One way is to read a scene in the play, and then read the Commentary for that scene. Keep on until you come to a test section, test yourself – then take a break. Or, read the Commentary for a scene, or several scenes, then read the scenes in the play, then go back to the Commentary.

Topics for Discussion, Brainstorming, and Revision gives topics that could well appear on exams or provide the basis for coursework. It would be particularly useful for you to discuss them with friends, or brainstorm them using Mind Map techniques (see p. xi).

How to Get an "A" in English Literature gives valuable advice on what to look for in any text, and what skills you need to develop in order to achieve your personal best. The Exam Essay is a useful night-before reminder of how to tackle exam questions, and the Model Answer and Essay Plans gives examples of an "A"-grade essay and other essay plans that you could expand into essays.

The questions

Whenever you come across a question in the guide with a star
✪ in front of it, think about it for a moment. You could even
jot down a few words to focus your mind. There is not usually
a "right" answer to these questions; it is important for you to
develop your own opinions if you want to get an "A." The Test
Yourself sections are designed to take you about 10–20
minutes each, which will be time well spent. Take a short
break after each one.

 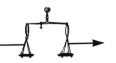

K EY TO ICONS

Themes

A **theme** is an idea explored by an author. Whenever a theme is dealt with in the guide, the appropriate icon is used. This means you can find where a theme is mentioned just by flicking through the book.

Go on – try it now!

Justice

Money and wealth

Love and friendship

Appearance and reality

Religion and race

Plots

Bond

Caskets

Elopement

Rings

 LANGUAGE AND STYLE

This icon is used in the Commentary wherever there is a special section on the author's choice of words and use of literary devices.

Location

Venice

Belmont

BACKGROUND

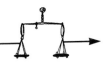

William Shakespeare wrote *The Merchant of Venice* in about 1597. It is regarded as a **comedy**, but it is also a serious moral drama.

To enjoy the play fully it helps to understand what life was like in England during the reign of Queen Elizabeth I. It was an age of maritime exploration, advances in understanding of the sciences, and religious tension between Protestants and Catholics. The common potato, which we take so much for granted today, had just been brought to England for the first time. Contrast this world with ours. Can you imagine life without airplanes, cars, computers, or space exploration? The development of such things changes our lives, the way we think, the attitudes we have, and even what we find amusing.

Values and attitudes

Although we must try hard to look at the play as the Elizabethans would have done, we are bound to bring the beliefs, values, and attitudes of our own time to the story. The character of Shylock gives us the best opportunity to explore differences between an Elizabethan and a modern response to the play. Just look at the way Shylock's character and religion are ridiculed. None of the characters respects his religious oaths and little tolerance is shown toward him. Ridiculing a stereotypical Jew was fashionable in Elizabethan drama because it reflected the commonly held view that Jews were to blame for everything from economic problems to child murdering and the plague. If Shakespeare had written the play today, he would be accused of anti-Semitism and inciting racial hatred.

Plots and themes

The main plot and several subplots in *The Merchant of Venice* were probably not Shakespeare's original ideas. It is more likely that he was inspired by medieval folk tales and wove them together into a new story.

POLITICS & COMMERCE

THE AGE OF

1580 - FRANCIS DRAKE BECAME FIRST ENGLISHMAN TO CIRCUMNAVIGATE THE WORLD

1586 - SIR WALTER RALEIGH IMPORTS TOBACCO FROM VIRGINIA

POTATO BROUGHT FROM COLOMBIA S. AMERICA

1587 - MARY QUEEN OF SCOTS (HALF SISTER OF ELIZABETH) EXECUTED AFTER FAILING TO RESTORE CATHOLICISM

QUEEN ELIZABETH I (1533 - 1603)

1588 - SPANISH ARMADA DEFEATED (129 SHIPS). ENGLAND DOMINATES THE SEAS

1605 - GUY FAWKES' GUNPOWDER PLOT TO BLOW UP HOUSES OF PARLIAMENT

1620 PILGRIM FATHERS BECOME FIRST ENGLISH SETTLERS IN NEW WORLD

THIS PERIOD IS ALSO KNOWN AS THE LATE RENAISSANCE, THE TERM USED TO DESCRIBE GREAT ADVANCEMENT OF KNOWLEDGE IN

SHAKESPEARE

ARTS AND SCIENCE

1579 - DEVELOPMENTS IN ALGEBRA AND OTHER BRANCHES OF MATH

FIRST GLASS EYES MADE

$$a + b^2$$

1582 - GREGORIAN CALENDER REPLACED WITH JULIAN IN EUROPE - USED EVER SINCE

1593 - PLAYWRIGHT CHRISTOPHER MARLOWE KILLED IN TAVERN BRAWL

WILLIAM SHAKESPEARE (1564-1616)

1594 - TINTORETTO'S DEATH FOLLOWS THAT OF OTHER GREAT ARTISTS LEONARDO, MICHELANGELO, AND RAPHAEL

GALILEO (1564-1642) MAKES GREAT ADVANCES IN PHYSICS, MATH, AND ASTRONOMY, IDEAS UNPOPULAR WITH CHURCH

1597 - IMPORTANT CHEMISTRY TEXTBOOK PUBLISHED (LIBAVIUS)

FIRST TELESCOPE (LIPPERSHEY)

SCIENCE, ART, NAVIGATION, AND COMMERCE. IT ENDED THE MIDDLE AGES AND BEGAN MODERN TIMES

1599 - FIRST SERIOUS WORK IN ZOOLOGY PUBLISHED (ALDROVANDI)

Whatever seems apparent is often contradicted in *The Merchant of Venice*. There is opposite evidence for most arguments, but its main message seems to be that higher qualities will always win over baser ones in the end. Justice should be tempered with mercy, and love, friendship, and generosity are higher qualities than hatred, revenge, and greed. Everyone gets what he or she deserves.

Try This

Make a list or Mind Map of things in your life that were not part of the lives and thoughts of English people in Elizabethan times. These headings may help you:

- Technology and industry
- The arts and entertainment
- Food, health, and medicine
- Clothes
- Travel

How else would life be different?

Now look through the book. Stop and read whatever catches your eye, then proceed in the order that suits you, in your own time.

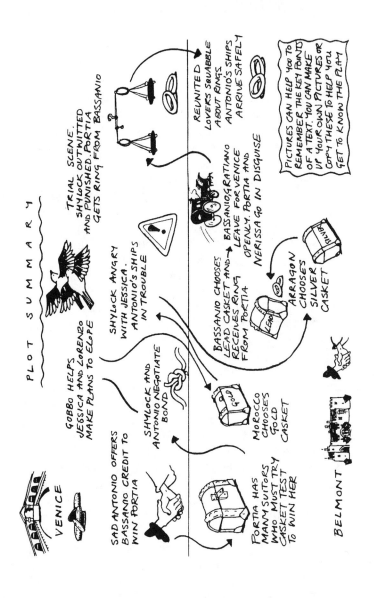

PLOT SUMMARY

VENICE

SAD ANTONIO OFFERS BASSANIO CREDIT TO WIN PORTIA

SHYLOCK AND ANTONIO NEGOTIATE BOND

GOBBO HELPS JESSICA AND LORENZO MAKE PLANS TO ELOPE

SHYLOCK ANGRY WITH JESSICA. ANTONIO'S SHIPS IN TROUBLE

TRIAL SCENE. SHYLOCK OUTWITTED AND PUNISHED. PORTIA GETS RING FROM BASSANIO

BELMONT

PORTIA HAS MANY SUITORS WHO MUST TRY CASKET TEST TO WIN HER

MOROCCO CHOOSES GOLD CASKET

BASSANIO CHOOSES LEAD CASKET AND RECEIVES RING FROM PORTIA

ARAGON CHOOSES SILVER CASKET

BASSANIO & GRATIANO LEAVE FOR VENICE OPENLY. PORTIA AND NERISSA GO IN DISGUISE

REUNITED LOVERS SQUABBLE ABOUT RINGS. ANTONIO'S SHIPS ARRIVE SAFELY

PICTURES CAN HELP YOU TO REMEMBER THE KEY POINTS OF A TEXT. YOU CAN MAKE UP YOUR OWN PICTURES OR COPY THESE TO HELP YOU GET TO KNOW THE PLAY.

5

Summary

Bassanio, a **scholar** and **soldier**, asks his friend **Antonio** (the "merchant of Venice" in the title) to lend him money to clear his **debts** and buy gifts to impress the wealthy Portia, whom he hopes to marry. Antonio has no spare **money** so he offers Bassanio his **credit** instead.

Portia considers the fairness of a test devised by her **father** before his death to determine who she will marry. Her husband will be the man who finds her **portrait** hidden inside one of three caskets – one made of gold, one of silver, and one of lead.

Bassanio asks **Shylock**, a moneylending Jew, for a loan of 3,000 ducats for three **months**, with Antonio's credit as security. Shylock hates all **Christians**, and particularly Antonio, because he often lends money for nothing. There seems to be no reason why Antonio will not be able to repay the loan, however, and Shylock is prepared to lend the money **without** charging interest. Almost as a joke, Antonio agrees to give Shylock a **pound** of his own **flesh** if he cannot pay on time.

Shylock's **daughter**, Jessica, elopes with her Christian lover, Lorenzo. She takes some of Shylock's **money** and gems with her. Shylock is **angry** when he finds out, and the news that Antonio's **ships** are wrecked increases his determination for revenge.

The Prince of Morocco chooses the **gold** casket, and the Prince of Arragon the **silver** one. Both fail to find the portrait. Bassanio correctly chooses the **lead** casket, and Portia gives him a **ring** as a token of her love. He promises not to part with it under any circumstances. Bassanio's friend, Gratiano, announces his intention to marry Portia's maid, **Nerissa**, and also receives a ring.

Antonio is resigned to losing his **life** to the vengeful Shylock but wants to see his friend before he dies. Portia urges Bassanio to go to **Venice** and see him. Portia and Nerissa pretend to go to a **monastery**, but Portia sends for legal help, and the two women also leave for Venice.

Antonio's case comes to court, and he is **defended** by Portia, disguised as a young lawyer. Despite all appeals, Shylock will not show **mercy** and forget the bond. Eventually, Portia uses a legal loophole to win Antonio's case. No **blood** is to be spilled, and the flesh taken must **weigh** exactly one pound.

Shylock is outwitted and **punished** for threatening to harm a Venetian citizen. He must give all his wealth to his daughter, Jessica, and her **husband** when he dies. In the meantime, Antonio is to be given half of the wealth to use, and hold in trust for Jessica. The final insult to Shylock is that he must become a **Christian**.

Portia and Nerissa, still in **disguise**, persuade the reluctant Bassanio and Gratiano to part with their **rings** as payment for winning the court case. When the lovers are reunited, they **squabble** about the rings, but all ends well and even Antonio's **ships** come safely back to port.

How much can you remember?

Try to fill in the words missing from this summary without looking at the original above. Feel free to use your own words if they have the same meaning.

Bassanio, a _____ and _____, asks his friend _____, (the "merchant of Venice" in the title) to lend him money to clear his _____ and buy gifts to impress the wealthy Portia, whom he hopes to marry. Antonio has no spare _____ so he offers Bassanio his _____ instead.

Portia considers the fairness of a test devised by her _____ before his death to determine who she will marry. Her husband will be the man who finds her _____ hidden inside one of three caskets – one made of gold, one of silver, and one of lead.

Bassanio asks _____, a moneylending Jew, for a loan of 3,000 ducats for three _____, with Antonio's credit as security. Shylock hates all _____, and particularly Antonio, because he often lends money for nothing. There seems to be no reason why Antonio will not be able to repay the loan, however, and Shylock is prepared to lend the money _____ charging interest. Almost as a joke, Antonio agrees to give Shylock a _____ of his own _____ if he cannot pay on time.

Shylock's _____, Jessica, elopes with her Christian lover, Lorenzo. She takes some of Shylock's _____ and gems with her. Shylock is _____ when he finds out, and the news that Antonio's ships are _____ increases his determination for revenge.

The Prince of Morocco chooses the _____ casket, and the Prince of Arragon the _____ one. Both fail to find the portrait. Bassanio correctly chooses the _____ casket, and Portia gives him a _____ as a token of her love. He promises not to part with it under any circumstances. Bassanio's friend, Gratiano, announces his intention to marry Portia's maid _____, and also receives a ring.

Antonio is resigned to losing his _____ to the vengeful Shylock but wants to see his friend before he dies. Portia urges Bassanio to go to _____ and see him. Portia and Nerissa pretend to go to a _____, but Portia sends for legal help, and the two women also leave for Venice.

Antonio's case comes to court, and he is _____ by Portia, disguised as a young lawyer. Despite all appeals, Shylock will not show _____ and forget the bond. Eventually, Portia uses a legal loophole to win Antonio's case. No _____ is to be spilled, and the flesh taken must _____ exactly one pound.

Shylock is outwitted and _____ for threatening to harm a Venetian citizen. He must give all his wealth to his daughter, Jessica, and her _____ when he dies. In the meantime, Antonio is to be given half of the wealth to use, and hold in trust for Jessica. The final insult to Shylock is that he must become a _____.

Portia and Nerissa, still in _____, persuade the reluctant Bassanio and Gratiano to part with their _____ as payment for winning the court case. When the lovers are reunited, they _____ about the rings, but all ends well and even Antonio's _____ come safely back to port.

Test yourself

? You will find the key point summary of *The Merchant of Venice* without the words beginning on page 7. Can you add the missing points in words using the pictures to help you?

now that you know the story, take a break before you find out who's who

PLOT SUMMARY

CAN YOU FILL IN THE BUBBLES?

VENICE

BELMONT

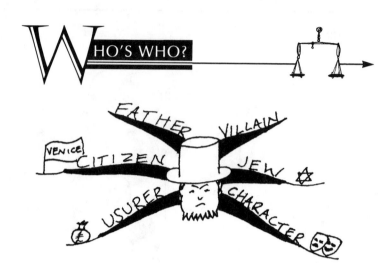

Shylock

Shylock, the moneylending Jew, is one of the most famous characters in English literature. He is usually regarded as a villain, but Shakespeare provides plenty of evidence to contradict a limited view of him.

Shylock's main qualification for villainy is that he refuses to release Antonio from the life-threatening bond. He has ample opportunity to accept in repayment much more money than he has lent out, but he insists on having his "pound of flesh." With Antonio dead, Shylock could raise the cost of borrowing to suit himself. His just claims on Antonio and his determination to have revenge provide the main story line and most of the dramatic tension.

Shakespeare presents Shylock as a mean, miserly stereotype of a Jew, at a time when it was quite usual to be anti-Semitic. On the face of it, Shylock is an obvious bad character, but there are reasons for his point of view, both as an individual and as a representative of a minority race.

Shylock the businessman

The very first words Shylock speaks say a lot about him as an individual. They are about money: *Three thousand ducats, well* (act 1, scene 3). To Shylock, ducats seem to be less important than revenge, although they seem to be as important to him as his daughter, Jessica. It may be fair for him to feel upset and angry with Jessica when she runs off with Lorenzo, but he behaves as if he cannot decide which loss is more important.

Shylock is also shrewd and artful. He is well informed about Antonio's various ships and their cargoes from the beginning of the play, and his craftiness is apparent in the way that he persuades Antonio to agree to the extremely sinister *merry bond* after they have discussed their differences openly. He shows his ability to think quickly in the trial scene (act 4, scene 1) after he has been outwitted. He tries to make the best of the situation on hearing about the loophole in the law by immediately saying: *I take this offer then. Pay the bond thrice/ And let the Christian go.*

Shylock the avenger

The worst part of Shylock's character shows in the trial scene. He will not show mercy toward Antonio despite all arguments and appeals from other Venetians who are all Christians. He refuses to send for a surgeon before he takes his pound of flesh because it is not in the bond, and the audience can almost feel his glee as he sharpens the knife.

Shylock the outsider

Shylock is an outsider who has been subjected to the mockery of Antonio, who lends money for favors without charging interest, whereas Shylock lends money to make his living. The friends have taunted him for his usury but are happy to use his services when they need them. Shylock is absolutely justified in claiming his bond as far as the law is concerned. He is not dishonest or dishonorable.

There is also some evidence to suggest that Shylock has some human feelings. He may be a killjoy who dislikes music and parties, and makes his daughter and servants unhappy, but he describes Lancelet as *kind enough* (act 2, scene 5, line 47). He also displays human feeling in act 3, scene 1 when he is goaded by Salerio and Solanio about Jessica's elopement. ✪ Can you find the words in the same scene that show he cared about his wife?

Shylock's real undoing is that he is actually prepared to kill Antonio – and in public. But Shakespeare provides some religious justification for his cruelty. By later saying: *An oath, an oath! I have an oath in heaven/ Shall I lay perjury upon my soul?* (act 4, scene 1), Shakespeare seems to make Shylock shift responsibility for his actions from himself and onto his religion. ✪ Do you think this suggests that Shylock needs to believe that his actions are justified on religious grounds to be able to see his savage oath through?

Just as Antonio and his friends represent all Christians and the majority view of society, Shylock represents all Jews and the minority view. He and his race have been persecuted throughout history, and have developed strong survival skills in a hostile world. ✪ Do you think Shylock is settling scores for all Jews?

Members of minority groups are sometimes prejudiced against the majority. ✪ What evidence is there to suggest whether or not Shylock is prejudiced against all Christians? (See Act 1, scene 3, line 42.)

At the end of the play we are left with a complex mixture of feelings. We feel sorry for Shylock at the same time we think he has received the treatment he deserves. We may think that taking his money away from him is appropriate punishment, but making him become a Christian after he has lost his servant and his daughter seems the ultimate insult and humiliation. Although he is defeated, he is not really sorry for his actions. He really cannot imagine life without money (act 4, scene 1, lines 390–393). Few of Shakespeare's characters could show better than Shylock that human nature is complex and that there is always another point of view.

What words?

?   Look at act 1, scene 3, lines 15–27. What do Shylock's words say about his ability to assess the risks Antonio is taking?

?   Why doesn't Shylock want to go out in act 2, scene 5?

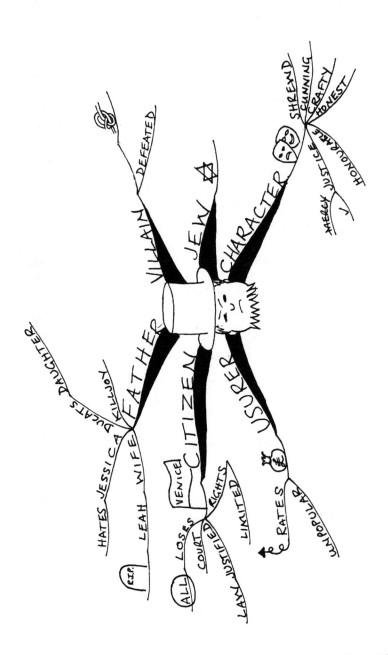

? Which passage in act 2, scene 8 suggests that Shylock may value his money more than his daughter?

? Read Shylock's speech in act 3, scene 1, lines 52–72. What is his argument for taking revenge?

Portia

In contrast to Shylock, Portia is a paragon of virtue. She is sensible, calm, coolheaded, and clever, and saves the day. She is a romantic figure who stands for just about everything that Shylock does not.

Portia the prize

For the first half of the play, Portia is presented as the rich and fair lady of Belmont pursued by many suitors. Shakespeare makes sure the audience appreciates her worth by making her the passive victim of a test with very serious rules. Any man attempting it must be prepared to leave immediately if he fails; he must never reveal the contents of the casket he chose or ask anyone to marry him again. Shakespeare spreads out the opening of the caskets by the three suitors over 11 scenes to increase her value as a prize.

She entertains the audience with witty character assassinations of her suitors, and later demonstrates what we now consider to be racial prejudice when she dismisses the Prince of Morocco in act 2, scene 7: *A gentle riddance. Draw the curtains, go./ Let all of his complexion choose me so.* (By *so*, she means "in this way," or fail to win her.)

Although her father is dead, his influence extends beyond the grave because he still holds control over Portia through the test. When Bassanio chooses the lead casket, she immediately passes into his control, and all her riches with her. This obedience is clearly meant by Shakespeare to be seen as a virtue. ○ You are reading the play 400 years after it was written. Do you think a daughter should obey *the will of a dead father*? What might his motives have been?

Portia saves the day

Portia becomes the dominant character in the play when she has secured a husband she loves and is told about Antonio's downfall. Thinking and acting quickly, she sends to Padua for legal advice, plans the trip to Venice, and invents a suitable cover story to conceal her absence from Belmont. Just in case the audience was in any doubt about Portia's qualities, Jessica praises her in act 3, scene 5. How does this prepare the audience for her performance in the trial scene that follows?

Portia is very impressive in the trial scene, although she has earlier described herself as *an unlessoned girl, unschooled, unpracticed.* Coolheaded throughout, she manipulates the course of events to allow Shylock every opportunity to relent. She would seem to prefer to win the case by appealing to the highest qualities human beings can hope to possess, which are so sadly lacking in Shylock. Only when all possibilities are exhausted does she fall back on the last resort of the law.

Women's issues

It is **ironic** that just as she is passed from father to husband with no control over herself, Portia is also robbed of the credit for her performance in court because she is disguised. Her courageousness throughout the trial demands calmness and confidence because it is a matter of life and death. It goes along with her modest nature that she should accept this lack of recognition, even though she alone, apart from the Duke, has thought to seek legal advice.

Just as Shakespeare manages to make the audience sympathize with a villain, he makes us admire a woman, although her gender is not revealed to the other characters. She is doing what before the late twentieth century would have been considered man's work, and her part would have been played by a boy actor. Perhaps Shakespeare secretly admires such qualities in a woman but has disguised them in a way that makes them acceptable to an Elizabethan audience.

What do you think?

? What do you think about someone in disguise with apparently no legal qualifications defending Antonio?

? How do you think the characters in the play would act if Portia defended Antonio's case dressed as a woman, not in disguise?

? Do you think Portia should show more mercy toward Shylock?

? Can you find Jessica's words in act 3, scene 5 that praise Portia? Taking particular note of imagery, how does her speech compare with Portia's speech beginning *The quality of mercy is not strained* (act 4, scene 1, line 190)?

Antonio

This is the pivotal character after whom the play is named. Antonio is *The Merchant of Venice* who really *hazards all he hath*. He has many excellent personal qualities, and is a loyal and generous friend. He is trustworthy, responsible, and a good Christian. To an Elizabethan audience, Antonio would indeed be the model gentleman.

From the opening lines of the play we understand that Antonio is prone to depression, because there is no apparent reason for his mood: *In sooth I know not why I am so sad.* His melancholy may be Shakespeare's way of giving the audience a hint of foreboding, or suggesting that Antonio has homosexual feelings for Bassanio. ✪ What do you think? He may be sad for himself because, as we soon learn, Bassanio has confided in him that he wants to tell him about a woman he intends to court.

Antonio can also be looked at as the ideal friend. He serves the best interests of others and offers Bassanio his credit without hesitation or reservation. Even after all the trouble he has experienced by helping Bassanio, he is ready to vouch for his friend's ability to keep Portia's ring safe in the final scene. When Antonio is sure he faces death, he asks nothing of

Bassanio but to see him before he dies.

Antonio's readiness to lend money without interest is the main reason why Shylock hates him so much. We do not witness Antonio *rating* Shylock, or calling him a dog as is claimed, but Antonio does not deny it, saying to Shylock, *I am as like/ To spit on thee again, to spurn thee too* (act 1, scene 3). ○ What does this say about Antonio?

As the plot develops, we witness the great courage and dignity with which Antonio faces what he thinks is certain death. His ability to be resigned and logical allows him to understand better than his friends that laws cannot be twisted, even in his unusual case. Antonio's readiness to spare Shylock's life when he is released from the bond supports Salerio's view that *A kinder gentleman treads not the earth* (act 2, scene 8). Do you think he considers the conditions he establishes at the end of the trial scene to be punishment enough?

If Shylock represents greed in this play, then Antonio represents its opposite, generosity. There are some similarities between them however. Both are businessmen, despite their different approaches. They are both alone in the world and without the romantic interest experienced by most of the other characters.

Over to you

? In productions of this play, Antonio is often played by an actor who is older than the other Venetian friends. Why do you think this is?

? Find Bassanio's lines (act 3, scene 2) that tell you where six of Antonio's *argosies* are.

? How do you think Antonio feels when all the lovers congregate in the garden in the final scene?

? How far is Antonio, like Shylock, an outsider?

Bassanio

Bassanio, *a Venetian, a scholar and a soldier*, is a lucky man. He is able to command great loyalty from his best friend, Antonio, and huge support from Portia when she becomes his wife. His attitude to life is carefree, and this has enabled him to live recklessly.

In his conversation with Antonio (act 1, scene 1, lines 122–141,) he explains that he has lived extravagantly and has pretended that he is better off than he actually is, so that he now owes money. ❂ What do you think this says about him?

Shakespeare seems to ask us to accept that Bassanio has good qualities without making him say or do very much to demonstrate them. The evidence of his good character mostly comes through the words and opinions of others. Nerissa first sings his praises and Portia replies that she remembers him *worthy of thy praise*. A servant in Portia's household further commends him, and we are left with little doubt about Bassanio's suitability as a husband for Portia. This is confirmed when he chooses the casket containing the portrait.

On the face of it, Shakespeare seems to be suggesting that Bassanio chooses the right casket because he has good judgment and knows the true value of things other than money, but we are presented with some contradictory evidence.

Bassanio has earlier said: *In Belmont is a lady richly left/ And she is fair* (act 1, scene 1, lines 168–169). ❂ How significant do you think it is that he mentions her money before her looks?

Bassanio speaks of Portia's *sunny locks* and compares her hair to a *golden fleece*, yet chooses the lead casket, even though he has borrowed from Antonio and put his life at risk, bought new uniforms for his servants, and hosted the masque (party), all in the hopes of impressing Portia and winning both her and her great fortune. Perhaps, therefore, it is an example of Shakespearean irony that he rejects the gold casket with the words: *Therefore thou gaudy gold/ I will none of thee* (act 3, scene 2).

Bassanio expresses many times all the things he would rather sacrifice than let Antonio lose his life (act 4, scene 1, lines 296–299), yet he never thinks to seek legal advice over the mess he has gotten Antonio into. By the end of the play, his debts are paid, he has won Portia, and he has seen his friend's life saved. The squabble over the ring seems to make him take life more seriously and we are left with the impression that he has matured and is now ready to take more responsibility for himself.

Now Try This

? What do you think of borrowing money to try to get more money?

? How would you sum up Bassanio's attitude toward marriage?

? Does Bassanio deserve a friend like Antonio?

? What sort of husband do you think Bassanio will make for Portia?

? What are the arguments for and against Bassanio giving the ring to the disguised Portia when she asks for it?

Jessica

Jessica is largely a device to bridge the gap between the Christians and the Jews by changing religion, and to draw some human feeling out of Shylock. By eloping with a Christian, she also helps fuel Shylock's anger so that he is all the more anxious to seek revenge on Antonio.

Jessica is not entirely a device, however, and she is not entirely good. In act 2, scene 5, line 46, she blatantly lies to Shylock. She also steals from him, and then spends wildly. She shows little remorse for deserting him. We must accept that her apparent lack of guilt about leaving her father is because he is such a killjoy, and a villainous man. ✪ How far do you think she is justified in her actions?

It is also interesting to compare Jessica with Portia. One obeys her father and the other does not. One's marriage is founded on a test of character in the man and of obedience in the woman. The other is based on breach of trust and stolen wealth.

Antonio's friends

Apart from Bassanio, Antonio has several friends. They share a common concern for their friend, but unlike Portia, seem unable to do anything practical to help.

Gratiano *speaks an infinite deal of nothing.* In contrast to Antonio he has a carefree nature and prefers not to worry about life. The purpose of his, and Nerissa's, presence in the play is to echo the romance between the aristocratic lovers, Bassanio and Portia.

Solanio and Salerio are little more than handlers of information; they often fill the gaps and tell the audience what is going on. They consider Antonio's sadness in act 1, scene 1, report Shylock's reaction to Jessica's elopement and wonder about its implications for Shylock's revenge, and bring the news of Antonio's plight to Belmont.

Lorenzo's significance stems mainly from being the Christian who marries Jessica – and benefits from Shylock's money.

Comic characters

There are several amusing scenes in *The Merchant of Venice*, but Lancelet Gobbo and his father, Old Gobbo, are the real comedians. In the funniest scene (act 2, scene 2), these two behave in the now well-established way of many comedy pairs. One is apparently cruel to the other, or makes fun of him because he is able to conceal certain information from the other, when really there is a great deal of affection between them.

Jessica describes Lancelet's character very well when she calls him *a merry devil* (act 2, scene 3, line 2). Just think of the way he teases his father with *confusions* in the previous scene. He is good company, a useful go-between for Jessica and Lorenzo, and brings to Shylock's house some relief from the *taste of tediousness*. His clowning does the same thing in the play by providing a break from the tension of the more dramatic scenes.

The comic characters also provide a taste of the lower class, and are a welcome change from princes, wealthy businessmen, and the aristocracy. They provide someone for ordinary members of the Elizabethan audience to identify with, and would have been among the most popular characters in the play.

Other characters

The **Duke of Venice** brings a sense of worldly authority and officialdom to the play, whereas Portia is the voice of moral authority. As an outsider, the duke has no vested interest in the outcome of the trial scene, and is therefore a fair judge.

As her mistress's confidante, **Nerissa** performs a useful service by allowing us to hear Portia's private thoughts about her suitors. With Gratiano, she reflects the central romance in a lowly way.

Tubal is apparently Shylock's only friend. He seems to be a device for supplying Shylock with news.

The **Princes of Morocco and Arragon** serve mainly to develop the plot of the caskets. They may be fine and honorable noblemen, but they do not have sufficient strength of character or judgment to make the right choice. Their failure builds up Portia's worth and confirms Bassanio's, because he does choose the right casket.

Test yourself

? Make a Mind Map of the characters and then list all the adjectives you can think of to describe each of them.

? Which characters do you most/least respect and why? Show this in Mind Map form.

? In act 5, when Lorenzo hears that he and Jessica have been awarded Shylock's wealth upon his death, he says: *you drop manna in the way of starved people.* In view of the riches they have already taken from Shylock and apparently spent wildly, what does this remark say about him?

? Draw a pie chart that includes all the characters. Divide the pie to reflect your view of the relative importance of each character.

now Take a break before you Tackle Themes

THEMES

A **theme** is an idea developed or explored throughout a work (such as a play, book, or poem). The main themes of *The Merchant of Venice* are shown in the Mini Mind Map above, and can be identified as follows:

- mercy and justice
- money and wealth
- love and friendship
- appearance and reality
- religion and race

Mercy and justice

When Portia says *mercy seasons justice* in the trial scene, she sums up the most important theme in the play. Look at her speech in which she appeals to Shylock to show mercy (act 4, scene 1, lines 190–212). She says that mercy cannot be forced from someone; it is a quality that must be freely given, and that ordinary human beings are seldom called upon to show. Mercy is a gift to wrongdoers from kings and rulers. This relates to an ancient idea that was still strongly believed by Elizabethans, that rulers are direct representatives of God on earth. They have a "Divine Right" and one cannot argue with them under any circumstances. Their authority and judgment are final.

Shakespeare explores the tension between justice and mercy through the attitudes of Shylock and Portia. Both are right. Shylock is justly entitled to his bond because it has been legally fixed and the terms agreed upon. On the other side of the scales is mercy. One minute justice overrides mercy, then suddenly the situation is reversed. ✪ How much mercy do you think Shylock is shown at the end of the trial?

An Elizabethan audience would probably think that the Venetians do show mercy to Shylock because they spare his life. They would probably have thought that by insisting on Shylock changing his faith, Antonio is offering salvation and is thus showing mercy. Shylock is taught the lesson that just as salt and pepper improve or season the flavor of food, so mercy seasons justice.

Note how Shakespeare presents the interplay between justice and mercy in the trial scene in a stylized rather than realistic way. He manages to make us think about these abstract qualities rather than practical details such as whether or not a trial is valid if the lawyer is in disguise.

Money and wealth

This is an important theme in the play. Most of the action springs from Bassanio's need for money and all the main characters are concerned with it in some way. The enmity between Shylock and Antonio is fueled by money, and their differing points of view about whether or not interest should be charged on loans explores a topical Elizabethan issue.

The rights and wrongs of money lending for profit were important to the Elizabethans. For centuries before the late 1500s, landowners and the aristocracy had controlled wealth, and to lend money for gain instead of doing so out of Christian charity was considered irreligious.

When Shakespeare wrote *The Merchant of Venice,* a new class of traders and businesspeople was emerging. With the new products, prices rose and the fortunes of the aristocracy began to decline. To finance business ventures, money had to be borrowed. Money lending for interest became legal in England in 1571, about 26 years before the play was written, but many more decades would pass before it lost its bad image. Since Jews and money lending were both disapproved of in Elizabethan England, a Shakespearean audience would start out with a poor opinion of Shylock.

Antonio represents the old, medieval view of money lending. He *lends out money gratis*, which annoys Shylock because it *brings down/ The rate of usance here with us in Venice*. Shylock represents the new. He uses *that which is mine own* to breed money, *the means whereby I live*.

The contrast in the way money lending is practiced between the Christian merchant and the Jew is echoed by Portia when she turns down payment for saving Antonio's life:

> *He is well paid that is well satisfied, / And I delivering you am satisfied, / And therein do account myself well paid; / My mind was never yet more mercenary.*
> (act 4, scene 1, lines 433–436).

Money lending is therefore an important economic issue throughout the play.

The relationship of the characters to money is also important. Miserliness and greed compel Shylock, Antonio is a merchant adventurer, Bassanio seeks money to clear debts and impress Portia, Jessica steals from her father, and though Portia is powerless over her fortune, it is significant that she has one. Antonio gets into trouble because of Bassanio's need for money, and it is interesting that Bassanio's first words about Portia are that she *is richly left*. Only after he says this does he mention her beauty.

The qualities of mercy, friendship, and generosity are juxtaposed with money, wealth, and greed throughout the play. Shakespeare's presentation of these themes ensures that we never really believe that Antonio's generosity toward Bassanio will be rewarded with a gory death, but we do want to know how he will be delivered from it. Shylock fails to understand higher human qualities so completely that he loses almost everything, including his own flesh and blood, Jessica. When she deserts him he says: *I would my daughter were dead at my foot, and the jewels in her ear! Would she were hearsed at my foot, and the jewels in her coffin* (act 3, scene 1). We are never quite sure whether his ducats or his daughter are more important to him. He is so miserly that we can feel him wince at the idea that Jessica should spend *fourscore ducats at a sitting.*

Location is also an important factor in the presentation of money and wealth in the play. Venice was an important and sophisticated center of trade and commerce in Shakespeare's time. The Rialto Bridge, mentioned several times by Shylock, is famous for hosting the city's business dealings.

The play is filled with imagery of wealth and riches. There are Shylock's ducats, the cargo of Antonio's ships, and the idea of the treasure they carry, which is echoed in the casket test. Shakespeare's handling of wealth also includes the idea of danger and risk that accompanies both Antonio's ships and the casket test.

Love and friendship

This theme runs throughout the text, in contrast to money and greed. The main love theme is carried through by the three pairs of lovers, of which Portia and Bassanio are the most important. Much drama and suspense surround their courtship due to the caskets test, and Shakespeare develops the plot so that we know Bassanio will make the right choice. Gratiano and Nerissa reflect the eloquent couple.

Jessica and Lorenzo are more complicated. Their purpose is mainly to provoke Shylock's revenge, and illustrate his lust for wealth. There is also the suggestion that it is possible for Jews to be admitted to Christian society if they cross the religious boundary and change faith as Jessica does willingly and as Shylock is forced to do.

Apart from the arrangements to elope being made in Venice, romantic love is advanced at Belmont, far away from the stresses and strains of city life. Images from Greek mythology describe Portia's beauty, and images of music signify harmony between the lovers, and at the end, of other matters.

The idea that friendship is more important than romantic love is demonstrated by the relationship between Antonio and Bassanio. So important is their friendship that, as he prepares to die, Antonio says:

Say how I loved you ... bid her be judge/ Whether Bassanio had not once a love.

To which Bassanio replies: *But life itself, my wife, and all the world/ Are not with me esteemed above thy life* (act 4, scene 1, lines 287–299).

Appearance and reality

This theme is suitably summed up by the message in the casket chosen by the first unsuccessful suitor – all that glisters (glitters) is not gold. The caskets plot demonstrates this most particularly. Each man must guess from the ambiguous message on each casket what is inside. Each interprets the message according to his own unique qualities, exactly as Portia's father had intended.

Arragon suspects that *all that glisters is not gold*, when he refers to *the fool multitude that choose by show, and which pries not to th'interior*. Bassanio says: *The world is still deceived with ornament.* In his long speech that follows (act 3, scene 2, lines 77–110), Bassanio considers this sly ability of things to be not what they seem, and how this truth is the undoing of many. He is appropriately rewarded for choosing "not by view."

Although the caskets demonstrate the theme of appearance and reality most obviously, we are introduced to the idea far earlier in the play when Shylock reveals in an aside his main motive for agreeing to lend Antonio the 3,000 ducats (act 1, scene 3, lines 41–52). This is not revealed to any of the characters in the play, although Antonio is fully aware that *the devil can cite Scripture for his purpose*. Antonio also juxtaposes appearance and reality when in the same speech he contrasts *evil soul* with *holy witness, a villain* with *a holy cheek,* and *a goodly apple rotten at the heart,* summing up with: *Oh what a goodly outside falsehood hath!*

Shylock's real motives are disguised in the one he pretends to have: *I would be friends with you and have your love/ Forget the shames that you have stained me with.*

Antonio at this stage in the play is prepared to see *much kindness* in the *gentle Jew*, but Bassanio is suspicious: *I like not fair terms and a villain's mind.*

Shylock's previous clever and cunning comment (act 1, scene 3) is calculated to make the two friends feel mean and small:
what these Christians are, / Whose own hard dealings teaches them suspect/ The thoughts of others!

The ultimate demonstration of things not being as they seem occurs in the trial scene when Portia disguises herself as the lawyer Balthasar. There is a further deception here for an Elizabethan audience, because not only would they be presented with a boy playing Portia, he would revert to himself when playing the lawyer. Nor would the rings plot work if the women were not in disguise to develop it.

Religion and race

Racial prejudice in *The Merchant of Venice* is focused on Shylock for being a Jew, and the Prince of Morocco for his dark skin. Religion and racial tension have always caused bitterness and inequality, and serious study of the play should consider how our values and attitudes have changed, and how this affects our view of the play.

We are studying the play only a relatively short time after the slaughter of six million Jews by the Nazis in World War II. This shocking holocaust was still so fresh in the minds of the people of Midland, Michigan, that in 1980, and earlier in New York State, *The Merchant of Venice* was banned because of the way Shakespeare presented Shylock.

More recently, apartheid, the racial segregation policy of the government of South Africa, has been dismantled after decades of bloodshed and upheaval. Our attitudes may be changing in the wake of these events, but in 1597, when the play was written, such discrimination was common. We cannot blame Shakespeare for reflecting the prevailing attitudes of his time, particularly because there is plenty of evidence in the play to show that he was not unsympathetic to Jews.

What did the Elizabethans have against the Jews?

There are several reasons for anti-Semitic feeling in England in Shakesperean times apart from an ancient tradition of hatred between Christians and Jews. In the early Middle Ages, Jews were accused of exploiting Christians, spreading the plague, and murdering babies. They were banned from England in 1290 and were not officially allowed back into the country until several decades after *The Merchant of Venice* was written, although a small community of Jews was known to exist in London in the late 1500s. These few were tolerated but little was known about them – they were not really part of Elizabethan life. This historical fact emphasizes Shylock's position as an outsider, exaggerated by his views on money lending, views long since accepted by banks, but disliked in Shakespeare's England.

A further reason for resentment toward Jews was that in 1593 Queen Elizabeth's Jewish doctor, Roderigo Lopez, was accused of trying to poison her. The trial was widely publicized and is thought to have inspired a popular revival of a play called *The Jew of Malta* by Shakespeare's contemporary, Christopher Marlowe. Marlowe's Jew, Barabas, however, evokes no sympathy. He is a villain with no saving graces whatsoever, unlike the complicated Shylock.

Shakespeare's sympathies

A moneylending Jew was clearly good for ticket sales in the Elizabethan theater, yet to say that Shakespeare was simply pandering to popular anti-Semitic feeling is too easy. Shylock's speech in act 1, scene 3, lines 116–139 not only gives the audience background information necessary for the development of the plot, but also outlines good reasons for Shylock to hate Antonio. He suggests to Antonio that he has a nerve to ask if he can borrow money when he has habitually scolded him, and accused him of being a *misbeliever, cut-throat dog.* Antonio has even spat at and insulted Shylock, who has borne it with patience and resignation.

Antonio does not deny Shylock's accusations. Instead he reinforces them: *I am as like to call thee so again/ To spit on thee again, to spurn thee too.* This is exactly the attitude to be expected from someone who believes himself to be superior, although Shylock's views on usury differ so greatly from Antonio's that they form the major reason for the opposition with which they face each other.

Ironically, Jews became money handlers largely because the prejudice of non-Jews kept them out of other jobs, and so Jews and money lending cannot be easily separated. Throughout history, Jews have been successful managers of money, a stereotype that continued into the twentieth century in the telling of so-called "Jewish jokes," which usually refer to someone who is stingy with money.

Shylock's *Hath not a Jew* speech (act 3, scene 1, lines 57–72) also points out that he is just as entitled to revenge as a Christian would be in the same situation. This makes the audience reflect on the matter and consider whether Shylock has some justification for his extreme position.

If Shakespeare had not meant his audience to question their attitude toward Jews or feel some sympathy for Shylock, it is difficult to understand why he included these speeches. It is also interesting to note that after Shakespeare has made Antonio insist on Shylock becoming a Christian, the final scene of the play opens with Lorenzo and Jessica, a Christian and a Jew, in harmony with each other. On the one hand this can be taken to mean that Shakespeare is saying that a Jew can only hope for salvation by becoming a Christian, as Jessica has done, and as Shylock has been forced to do. On the other hand, he may be saying that unity and equality are possible between people with great differences. ✪ What do you think?

The Prince of Morocco

We learn a little about the Elizabethan view of race from the interaction between Portia and the Prince of Morocco. We are prepared for the exchange from as early as act 1, scene 2, when Portia speaks of a suitor who may have *the complexion of a devil.* A modern black Prince might not acknowledge that anyone would think that black people are inferior to white, but Shakespeare makes Morocco anticipate Portia's response:

Mislike me not for my complexion/ The shadowed livery of the burnished sun/ To whom I am a neighbor and near bred (act 2, scene 1, lines 1–3).

He shows pride when he goes on to say:

I would not change this hue/ Except to steal your thoughts, my gentle queen.

At the end of act 2, scene 7, after Morocco has chosen the wrong casket and left, Portia concludes their meeting with: *A gentle riddance. Draw the curtains, go./ Let all of his complexion choose me so.* ✪ These lines are frequently left out of productions. Why do you think this is done? Should we examine our own prejudices? Should such lines be left out in order to not offend anyone?

Test yourself

? Think about the quality of mercy. Should it be shown to wrongdoers?

? Divide this circle into pieces of pie that reflect the relative importance of each of the themes as you see it. The theme you consider to be most important should be the largest piece. Are there any other themes in the play you would like to add?

? Using these pictures to help you, add words to describe the themes they represent:

now take a break before you look at Shakespeare's language

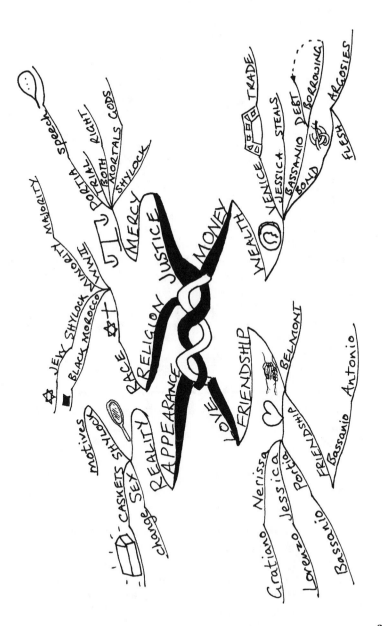

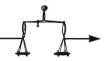

LANGUAGE, STYLE, AND STRUCTURE

Can you think of times when you use different types of language? For example, you probably use words with friends that you would not use with a teacher or a parent. In the same way, Shakespeare varies the language he gives his characters according to who they are, who they are speaking to, and what about. *The Merchant of Venice* is written in a mixture of verse and prose.

Prose

Prose is flowing writing with no particular rules. It is conversational and less formal than verse. In Shakespeare, prose is used by characters such as Gobbo who are lowly servants rather than educated gentlefolk. Portia, an aristocratic character, uses verse most of the time, and certainly on formal occasions. She does use prose, however, when she is talking informally and confidentially with Nerissa.

Solanio, Salerio, and Shylock usually use verse, but in act 3, scene 1 they all use prose, probably because they are discussing serious matters. Solanio's and Salerio's speech loosens up to reflect confidentiality, and Shylock's exchanges with Tubal are emotional rather than measured and formal.

Verse

Shakespeare's formal language, called **blank verse**, is rather like poetry. It has a regular rhythm created mainly by the way words with different numbers of syllables are joined together and how words or sounds are repeated.

Blank verse has a tighter structure than prose. Most of the lines are regular, and they consist of five **iambic feet**. An **iambus** is a foot of two syllables:
The qual/ ity/ of mer/cy is/ not strain'd/ (act 4, scene 1, line 190).

❂ How many syllables are there in this line? Now choose a speech in which the verse looks regular, and tap the beat while saying it aloud. How many beats are there to each line? Then choose a speech written in prose. Does it have the same consistent number of beats?

Now look at the first scene. Although they are discussing personal matters, Antonio's friends use the formal verse that is to be expected from educated "young men about town" of some social standing.

If you look at the last two lines of most of the scenes, you will see that they rhyme. The **rhyming couplet,** as it is called, at the end of scenes has the added advantage of warning the audience that the scene is ending, and it will be okay to cough or shift position.

Imagery

Imagery is the use of words to create pictures, or images, in the viewer's or reader's mind. Imagery makes what is being said more effective, can make an idea more powerful, and can help create a mood. You will find examples of imagery on almost every page of Shakespeare. Images of animals, storms, and water are common in The Merchant of Venice.

Animal imagery is often used both by Shylock and others to describe him. We learn that Antonio has often referred to him disparagingly as *dog,* and he is also compared to the devil to reinforce his wickedness. Shylock first brings up the idea of sheep when he tells a Bible story to illustrate his views on usury (act 1, scene 3, lines 79–98). As if they had been present during this conversation, Shakespeare makes several of the other characters pick up the sheep imagery again, particularly to call Shylock a wolf preying on Antonio, who is compared – by himself and others – to a sheep. Look at Antonio's speech in act 4, scene 1, lines 71–84, and Gratiano's in lines 130–140.

✪ Can you pick out the images of sheep and wolves?

The **watery** images reflect the canals of Venice, and echo the idea of ships abroad. The rough seas, wind, and storms, and especially how ships fare in them are much talked about in Venice, as they probably would have been in Elizabethan London. **✪** Look at the first scene, up to line 41. How many watery images can you pick out?

When Bassanio first tells Antonio about Portia, he uses references to the sea. Belmont itself lies a sea voyage away from Venice, and the Prince of Morocco also refers to the sea when he tries to win Portia.

The storms of Venice contrast with **music** at Belmont. Music is a symbol of love and harmony, and it is no accident that a song is sung as Bassanio chooses the winning casket. When Lorenzo and Jessica talk of music in the garden at Belmont, all has turned out well. Not surprisingly, Shylock hates music. He wants Jessica to lock up the house when she hears *the drum/ And the vile squealing of the wry-necked fife.*

Look at Lorenzo's speech in act 5, scene 1, lines 78–97. It is a veiled reference to Shylock in the way it contains images that refer to the power music has to tame beasts: *The man that hath no music in himself,/ Let no such man be trusted.*

Images of **money, riches, and treasure** adorn many of the speeches used to develop the bond plot and the caskets subplot.

Now Try This

?
?
?

Find an example of a rhyming couplet.
Who in the play uses prose and why?
Which of the following is written in iambic feet?
If it please you to dine with us.
For if I do, I'll mar the young clerk's pen.

now take a break before we talk about style

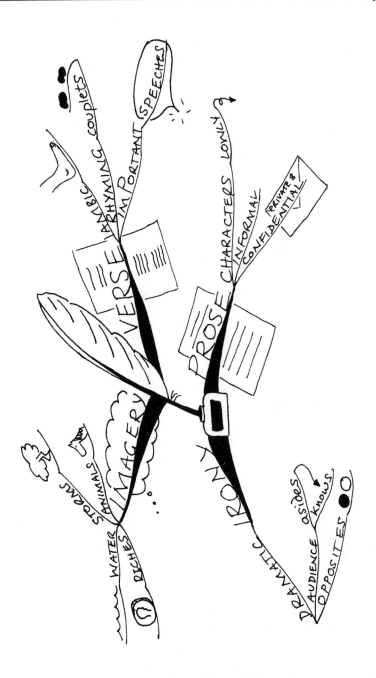

Setting and atmosphere

  All the action in the play takes place in Venice or at Belmont. What goes on in each place is significant.

For several centuries before Shakespeare wrote the play, Venice had been an important commercial center, and a place of learning and culture. It was a sophisticated city with canals rather than roads. To an Elizabethan audience it would have seemed extremely exotic and picturesque. Among its famous bridges were the Rialto, renowned for trade, and the Bridge of Sighs, which was the way to prison. It is not surprising therefore that matters relating to money, trade, and law are dealt with in what is very much the "man's world" of Venice.

By contrast, Belmont, meaning "beautiful mountain," is an imaginary haven in the countryside far away from the city life of Venice. Mountains imply high, lofty ideals, and it is fitting that Belmont should be Portia's home. It offers a traditionally "feminine" atmosphere with its peace, tranquility, and harmony. With the exception of the planning of the elopement between Jessica and Lorenzo, all the romantic developments take place at Belmont.

The final scene of the play is set to music in the garden at Belmont, and all the lovers meet and develop their relationships there. Gardens, like music, were very much symbols of harmony and romance in classical Greece and Rome, an idea that was picked up and continued in English poetry and literature, especially during the age of Shakespeare.

Irony

Irony is used in the plot as a device in language and to give the audience the advantage of more knowledge than the characters have. Irony occurs when the opposite of what is meant is said, or when something turns out in the opposite way to what is intended. An example of irony in the plot is the way that a thing of great worth, such as Portia's portrait, is concealed in the casket of least apparent value.

One example of irony in language is when Lancelet Gobbo says: *I cannot get a service, no! I have ne'er a tongue in my head* (act 2, scene 2, lines 155-156).

He means that he cannot get a job because he is too quiet, when in reality he talks a great deal and is perfectly capable of finding work. In act 1, scene 3, Shylock refers to the *merry bond* he has made with Antonio. ❏ Why is this description of the bond ironic?

Dramatic irony arises when the audience, and perhaps some of the characters, know something that other characters do not. This helps to build suspense, and give hints about what will happen next. Think about the way that Shylock's **aside** (act 1, scene 3, lines 41–52) reveals his true motives for lending money to Antonio. Because an aside is witnessed only by the audience, Shakespeare makes sure we know more than the Christians so that we will become involved in the play, watch for signs of Shylock's revenge, and want to see what happens.

Further examples of dramatic irony include the way that we know of the attraction between Portia and Bassanio before they confirm it to each other. Along with Portia and Nerissa, we also know the contents of the caskets by the time Bassanio takes his turn, and that Jessica is planning to leave her father without him knowing. Blind Old Gobbo becomes the butt of a joke because he is teased by his son, but we can see what is going on.

The most important example of dramatic irony can be found in the trial scene. Only we know that Balthasar and his clerk are really Portia and Nerissa in disguise. The way that they later tease their husbands for giving up the rings amuses us because, like Old Gobbo, the men have less information than we do. ❏ Why do you think Shakespeare abandons dramatic irony to make Portia's revelation about the loophole in the law come as a surprise to the audience as well as to all the characters?

Comedy

Unlike most other Shakespearian comedies, *The Merchant of Venice* deals with serious moral issues that make it inconsistent with the usual conventions of comedy. Complex villains such as Shylock are more usually found in tragedy. Nonetheless, Shakespearian comedy usually has these characteristics:

- the ability to make the audience laugh or feel happy
- silliness, such as girls dressing up as boys
- unlikely coincidences or happenings
- one or more characters being the butt of the jokes
- **puns** or plays on words
- the audience knowing more than some or most of the characters (dramatic irony)
- usually a happy ending – no one dies
- the assumption that "good" characters won't be harmed.

✪ Check the ones that you think apply to *The Merchant of Venice*. Think of an example in the play for some of the statements you have checked.

✪ Is there a TV comedy show that you find funny? Does it share any of these characteristics?

Structure and plot

In literature, **structure** refers to the framework for piecing the parts of the work together. The word **plot** usually means the whole story. However, in *The Merchant of Venice,* it is useful to think of the separate threads of the overall plot as separate plots that weave around each other.

Act 1 sets the scene and introduces most of the plots, themes, and characters. Act 2 develops the plots and themes and reveals more about the characters, and their relationships. We are becoming involved and want to know what will happen next. By act 3, the caskets subplot is resolved and the rings subplot is introduced, but Shakespeare does not allow us to relax for long without creating more suspense. He does this by reminding us of Antonio's problem with the bond. The play reaches its climax in act 4 when the trial scene resolves the main plot. Act 5 ties up the romantic subplots and loose ends.

The bond

This is the focal point of the main plot; it is introduced early in the play. How other factors and events come to bear on the bond and the threat it poses to Antonio's life is made clear to the audience in act 2. In act 3 the situation is so serious that Antonio's death seems inevitable, and in act 4 the tables turn, there is a climax, and the plot is resolved.

The caskets

The caskets test is also an important plot. It is interwoven with the bond plot until it is resolved by Bassanio choosing correctly before the trial scene takes place. Short scenes dart between Venice and the bond and Belmont and the caskets in act 2. Developing both plots at the same time creates pace and suspense, but some directors rearrange or omit some of these scenes. ✪ Do you find the caskets plot believable?

! ! ! Remember the orders in which the suitors try their luck by using the word **MAB**: Morocco, Arragon, Bassanio. The order of the caskets is easy to remember, because they descend in value: gold, silver, lead. The Prince of Morocco, a sunny country, chooses gold, a yellow, "sunny" metal.

The elopement

Jessica's elopement with Lorenzo forms a subplot. It has more significance as something affecting other characters and events than it has in itself, although it contributes to the love theme. The elopement feeds the bond plot by adding fuel to Shylock's need for revenge against Antonio. In act 5 it demonstrates that reconciliation between Jews and Christians is possible. The disobedient couple who have done many wrong things also provide material for comparison with Portia and Bassanio.

The rings

This subplot is not introduced until act 3. It is mainly a comic device to entertain and provide light relief for the audience after the seriousness of act 4, scene 1. Ending the play with romance and little squabbles over rings, after all the characters have been through, rounds things off and brightens the mood of the audience so that they go home feeling lighthearted and entertained. There is a serious aspect to the rings, however. They echo the idea of bonds and oaths, and pose difficult dilemmas for Bassanio and Gratiano to resolve.

Picture this

? Look at this graph and see how the rings subplot is introduced in act 3, scene 2, develops in act 4, scene 1, and peaks in act 5, scene 1. When the rings plot is not developing, the line is level.

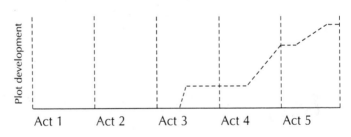

--- = development of the rings subplot

Using different-colored pens, draw in the other plots in the same way.

? Fill in the blanks in the following speech (act 1, scene 3). The missing words are listed below the speech, in the wrong order. (For a tougher test, try it without looking at the list!)

Signor _____, many a time and _____

In the Rialto you have _____ me

About my_____ and my _____.

Still I have _____it with a _____shrug,

For _____ is the badge of all our _____.

You call me _____, cut-throat dog,

And _____ upon my _____ gaberdine,

And all for _____ of that which is _____ own.

Jewish	mine	patient	rated	Antonio
moneys	oft	sufferance	borne	usances
use	spit	misbeliever	tribe	

? Comment on the imagery of Bassanio's speech (act 1, scene 1) in which he tells Antonio of his intention to mend his ways.

now for a running commentary – after the break

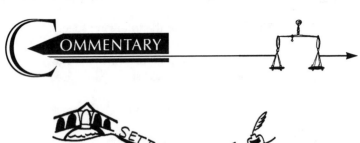

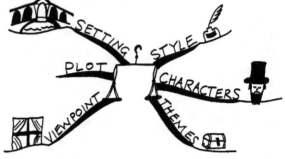

The Commentary looks at each scene in turn, beginning with a brief preview that will prepare you for the scene and help in last-minute review. The Commentary discusses whatever is important in the scene, focusing on the areas shown in the Mini Mind Map above.

Wherever there is a focus on a particular theme, the icon for that theme appears in the margin (see p. xv for key). Look out, too, for the "Style and Language" sections. Being able to comment on style and language will help you to get an "A" on your exam.

You will learn more from the Commentary if you use it alongside the play itself. Read a scene from the play, then the corresponding Commentary section, or the other way around.

Remember that when a question appears in the Commentary with a star ✪ in front of it, you should stop and think about it for a moment. And remember to take a break after completing each exercise!

Act 1 *scene* 1

◆ Antonio, the merchant of Venice, discusses possible reasons for his sadness with friends Salerio and Solanio.
◆ Bassanio, Gratiano, and Lorenzo are introduced.
◆ Antonio and Bassanio confirm their friendship.

◆ Bassanio tells Antonio that he intends to woo Portia.

◆ Antonio offers to help Bassanio clear his debts by letting him use his credit.

By opening with an examination of the reasons for Antonio's sadness, Shakespeare is setting the tone for future developments in the play. The sadness seems to have no cause, and so the audience is given a hint that something will go wrong. Looking for reasons for the sadness is also a convenient way for Shakespeare to tell us how highly Antonio is regarded by his friends, and to make sure we know all about his business interests.

We learn that there are many risks and worries facing a merchant whose assets are at sea, but that the risks can be reduced by spreading merchandise among different ships. All the main developments in the play arise from this calculated risk that Antonio is taking, and the possibility of disaster.

By leaving Antonio and Bassanio alone together to have a confidential conversation, the audience is made aware of the close friendship between them (lines 137–146). ✪ Why do you think Shakespeare makes sure we know these two are such great friends?

Scene 1 closes with a sense of foreboding. No explanation for Antonio's sadness has been given, fortunes can be lost in the treacherous sea, Bassanio wants to woo Portia, *a lady richly left* (line 168), but has debts instead of assets, and Antonio offers *what my credit can in Venice do*, assets that are not secure.

Shakespeare captures his audience's attention by giving the play an exotic setting that contrasts greatly with Elizabethan England. He also refers to the romantic fantasy world of Greek mythology. Bassanio compares the wooing of Portia to the myth of Jason and the Golden Fleece to convey to Antonio how great a prize she is (lines 172–183).

Act 1 *scene* 2

◆ The audience is introduced to Portia and her maid, Nerissa.

◆ The rules of the caskets test that Portia's suitors must undertake are introduced.

◆ Portia scorns the suitors.

◆ Nerissa reminds Portia of Bassanio. They agree that he would be *the best deserving of a fair lady*.

Like Antonio in the previous scene, Portia is feeling gloomy. She tells us how unhappy she is about the lack of control she has over choosing a husband, and questions the fairness of a test her father has devised to decide for her.

Nerissa comforts and reassures Portia that her father has set her suitors a wise and fair test. She says that only a man with the right personal qualities will be able to guess which one of the three caskets of gold, silver, and lead hides the winning portrait of Portia.

Shakespeare breaks up the serious conversations that have taken place so far by entertaining the audience with Portia's witty and scornful comments about her suitors. She makes fun of noblemen from different countries in a way that was probably meant to entertain the audience with topical jokes about stereotypes of foreigners.

Shakespeare also keeps us interested by making sure that we know more about the mutual interest between Bassanio and Portia than the characters know themselves.

By the close of the scene, the subplot of the caskets is established, we understand the nature of the challenge Bassanio will be faced with, and we suspect that Portia would prefer Bassanio to any of her other suitors.

Portia shares her secrets with Nerissa, far away from the sophisticated city of Venice. Shakespeare has written their informal conversation in prose to emphasize the confidentiality between them; it shows that they are comfortable with each other.

Images of money and riches are often used in *The Merchant of Venice*. The three chests echo the idea of exotic treasures away at sea, and both Portia's and Antonio's riches are surrounded by risk.

Now Try This

? Who *speaks an infinite deal of nothing*?
? Find the lines in scene 1 that show Bassanio has debts

and has pretended to be better off than he actually is.

? At this stage in the play, do you share Nerissa's confidence in the caskets test as a good way to find the right husband for Portia?

Act 1 *scene* 3

- Bassanio and Shylock discuss the terms of the loan — 3,000 ducats for three months.
- We discover that Shylock is a committed Jew who hates Christians, especially Antonio.
- Shylock exposes the double standard — Antonio criticizes him for usury, but is happy to use the service when he needs it.
- Antonio enters into a bond on Bassanio's behalf; he agrees to give up a pound of flesh if he cannot repay the loan on time.

This is a key scene because it establishes the main plot – the bond between Shylock and Antonio. The character of Shylock is also firmly established by the information we are given about his religion, profession, and vengeful attitude. He sees the bond as an opportunity to *feed fat the ancient grudge* (line 47) he bears Antonio.

It is important that Shakespeare makes Shylock expose Antonio's double standard. It shows that people who have a different religion, or have values that are different from those around them, are often victims of prejudice and criticism. This is the basis of the anti-Semitism that Jews have experienced from non-Jews for so long. Shylock sees the profit he makes from his business as *well-won thrift.* He suggests that Antonio sees it as interest (lines 51–52). We begin to see some justification for Shylock's meanness, and consider Antonio from his enemy's viewpoint.

A loan of 3,000 ducats for three months is agreed on. Instead of paying interest if the loan is not then repaid, Antonio agrees *in merry sport* (line 157) to forfeit a pound of flesh. At the end of the scene, in which we have heard Shylock's private and malicious thoughts, Bassanio says: *I like not fair terms and a villain's mind* (line 192). ✪ What does this statement mean, and how does it add to the sense of foreboding?

Shakespeare makes sure the audience does not miss the very important terms of the bond at the beginning of this scene. He makes Shylock repeat each detail one by one, and then links the separate points saying: *Three thousand ducats for three months, and Antonio bound* (lines 1–10).

The use of prose for the conversation between Bassanio and Shylock in the opening lines of scene 3 suggests informality, even though the subject of their discussion is the loan, a formal arrangement. Making his enemy feel at ease is a clever way for Shylock to sell his services. Shakespeare returns to blank verse to emphasize the more formal relationship between Shylock and Antonio.

We are given some important information about Shylock's motives for agreeing to the bond in an "aside," a speech revealing a character's inner thoughts to the audience only (lines 41–52). ❍ Why do you think Shakespeare makes Shylock reveal more to the audience about his private thoughts than he does to the other characters?

Test yourself

? Who says *Why look you, how you storm!* and who is being spoken to?

? How does Shylock's tone change from when he begins his speech *Signor Antonio ...* (line 116) to the end of the scene?

? At this point in the play, does it seem that Antonio will be able to repay the loan? What do the characters say and do to make you think this?

now treat yourself to a break before the act with many scenes

Act 2 scene 1

◆ Prince of Morocco arrives at Belmont.
◆ More detail about the caskets test is given.

The act opens with the Prince appealing to Portia not to dislike him because his skin is darker than hers. This reminds us that racial prejudice – not just religious prejudice – is an issue here.

Portia makes it clear that the rules of the test are binding
regardless of all other considerations. The formal conversation
that follows reveals that any suitors wishing to undertake the
test must do so very seriously. Any man who fails can never
speak to lady afterward/ In way of marriage. This builds up
tension in the play because the stakes are so high.

Act 2 *scene* 2

◆ Shylock's discontented servant, Lancelet Gobbo, is
  introduced.
◆ Lancelet plays games with his blind father, Old Gobbo.
◆ Bassanio agrees to Lancelet's request to serve him instead of
  Shylock.
◆ Gratiano tells Bassanio he wants to go to Belmont. Bassanio
  agrees but warns him that he must behave appropriately.

In contrast to the previous scene, here we meet the opposite end
of the social scale in the character of Lancelet Gobbo. He is a
simple servant whose opening speech relieves the mounting
tension as he debates with himself whether or not to leave
Shylock's service. By calling Shylock a fiend, *a kind of devil,*
and *the very devil incarnation,* he is also helping to build up the
audience's understanding of Shylock as a villain.

The mischievous Lancelet entertains the audience by
teasing his father, who has a present of a *dish of doves*
for Shylock. In an aside Lancelet tells us he will *try confusions*
with the blind old man. After giving his father muddled directions
to Shylock's house, he encourages him to talk about his son, and
then tells him he is dead. When Lancelet reveals the truth, the
old man does not believe him at first. They are soon united in the
successful mission to find Lancelet a new master in Bassanio.

Although no reason is given, Gratiano presses Bassanio to be
allowed to go to Belmont with him. Bassanio agrees but tells
Gratiano that he must behave modestly rather than wildly. What
are his reasons for concern (lines 181–191)? ❍ Do you think
Bassanio is wise to agree?

 As lowly characters, Lancelet and his father speak in a
wordy prose style instead of speaking in the formal verse

that is usually reserved for characters who are educated and of high social standing. Bassanio, for example, speaks in verse throughout the scene.

The trick Lancelet plays on his father is typical of the way in which a comic might entertain an audience at the theater. They know more than the old man and feel sorry for him, but at the same time they know the teasing is harmless fun, which makes them laugh. Shakespeare further develops the humor by having both father and son make Lancelet's case to Bassanio in a deliberately long-winded way, even though they both state that they will come straight to the point. ❂ Exactly which of their words state this?

❂ Do you think that jokes at a blind man's expense would be acceptable in a modern play? Do you think Lancelet is at all cruel?

Act 2 *scene* 3

◆ Jessica is introduced; she asks Lancelet to secretly deliver a letter to Lorenzo.
◆ A plot for Jessica to marry Lorenzo, a Christian, is revealed.

In this short scene, Jessica expresses her sorrow that Lancelet is leaving her father's employment. He has been good company and they are sorry to part. Jessica's trust in Lancelet is revealed when she asks him to deliver the letter to Lorenzo without Shylock knowing.

A second love affair is introduced as we learn that Jessica intends to become a Christian if Lorenzo keeps his promise to marry her. The position of Shylock as the play's villain is again confirmed by Jessica briefly asking herself why she is *ashamed to be my father's child.* Her intention to marry a non-Jew further isolates Shylock from all the other characters.

A sense of anti-Semitism is countered by Lancelet calling Jessica *Most beautiful pagan, most sweet Jew,* which suggests that a person's nature can override other objections.

Act 2 *scene* 4

◆ Friends prepare for the party.
◆ Lancelet gives Jessica's letter to Lorenzo.

♦ Lorenzo tells Lancelet to confirm to Jessica that he will not fail her.

♦ Lorenzo tells Gratiano of the plan to elope with Jessica.

This scene advances the subplot of the romance between Jessica and Lorenzo by revealing that Jessica loves Lorenzo, giving details of their elopement plan, and showing that Lorenzo believes it is justified.

Over to you

?   Gratiano does not say why he wants to go to Belmont. Why do you think he does?

?   Who receives Old Gobbo's present, and what is it?

?   Draw Mind Maps of two of the characters from what you know about them at this point in the play.

Act 2 *scene* 5

♦ Shylock is reluctant to dine with the Christians.

♦ Shylock tells Jessica to lock up the house while the public party goes on.

♦ Lancelet secretly delivers Lorenzo's message to Jessica.

The pace of the plot quickens in this scene. Shakespeare is building up suspense about the elopement by continuing brief, secret, and important exchanges between the characters. Arrangements for the elopement are progressing smoothly. Only the audience is fully aware of what is going on, although Shylock senses the conspiracy. ✪ Find the lines that indicate this.

Shylock repeats his poor opinion of the Christians and the same reluctance to dine with them that he expressed in act 1. This reinforces the theme of religious hatred and prepares the audience for how badly Shylock will react to Jessica's elopement.

Note the joke that Lancelet has at Shylock's expense in lines 9–10. He impudently answers back when Shylock tells him he did not have permission to call Jessica.

Jessica's blatant lie to her father is another example of reality being different from appearance.

Act 2 *scene* 6

♦ Gratiano and Salerio discuss the impatience of new lovers.
♦ Jessica and Lorenzo confirm their love and elope.
♦ Bassanio and Gratiano leave for Belmont.

Lorenzo is late for his meeting with Jessica and the party (masque), which creates more suspense and gives Shakespeare an opportunity to make Gratiano and Salerio think about love and human nature. They say that new lovers are seldom late and that romantic enthusiasm dulls with time.

Jessica in the disguise of a boy gives Lorenzo a casket containing money and leaves Shylock's house taking more wealth with her. Shakespeare prepares us for a return to Belmont and the caskets test when Antonio tells Gratiano that they must prepare to set sail.

Act 2 *scene* 7

♦ Prince of Morocco chooses the gold casket and fails to win Portia.

The scene switches from the intrigues of Venice to the haven of Belmont. In a long and formal speech, the Prince considers the puzzling inscriptions on each casket. Seduced by appearance, he picks gold. It does not contain Portia's portrait, and so the Prince's *suit is cold.* When the Prince has left, Portia makes it clear that she is glad he made the wrong choice. She adds: *Let all of his complexion choose me so,* revealing what she really feels about being courted by someone with a darker skin color.

Note the short poem contained in the gold casket, lines 73–81. The last word of every line rhymes with "gold."

Act 2 *scene* 8

♦ Salerio and Solanio discuss Shylock's reaction to Jessica disappearing with his money and precious stones.
♦ They show concern for Antonio's ships and the bond he has made with Shylock.

This scene advances the plot and reminds the audience about the bond. We learn that Bassanio and Gratiano have sailed without Lorenzo, who has been seen in a gondola with Jessica. In a speech designed to amuse the audience, Solanio describes Shylock's anger that Jessica has left with his riches. The conversation becomes more serious as Solanio points out that Jessica's elopement with a Christian will make Shylock all the more determined to have his bond if Antonio cannot pay up on time. The friends are further concerned about an Italian ship wrecked in the English Channel in case it is Antonio's.

The scene closes with a discussion about Antonio's kind character and love for his friend, Bassanio.

Look at Solanio's description of what *the dog Jew did utter in the streets* (lines 12–23). The speech provides a good example of **alliteration**, the repetition of the same sound at the beginnings of words. ✪ Which sound (and letter) is repeated in this example?

Act 2 *scene* 9

◆ The Prince of Arragon unsuccessfully tries to win Portia by choosing the silver casket.
◆ Bassanio is about to arrive to try his luck with the caskets test.

Act 2 closes in the formal setting of Belmont. The Prince of Arragon's failed attempt to win Portia clears the way for Bassanio. Before he chooses the silver casket, the Prince reminds the audience of the three strict conditions of the test to illustrate how it should not be taken lightly.

✪ Find the lines that tell you what the three conditions are.

The Prince departs and a messenger arrives with news of another, more impressive suitor soon to be expected. Nerissa hopes, and the audience knows, that this will be Bassanio.

Shakespeare has developed the plot so that only Portia, her servants, and the audience have witnessed the unsuccessful attempts of the two princes to choose the casket that contains

Portia's portrait. We are fairly sure that Shakespeare has engineered events so that it will be found in the lead casket by Bassanio, but we want to see it happen. This is a clever way of keeping the audience interested.

Now Try This Test

? Where has an Italian ship been wrecked, and who might it belong to?

? Which words of Arragon's show that he understands appearances can deceive, even though he makes the wrong choice?

? Write the names Shylock, Antonio, and Bassanio down one side of a piece of paper. Next to each, write any of the following adjectives that describe them. Try to think of reasons for your choice.

**honest   two-faced   arrogant   prejudiced
irresponsible   miserable   generous   friendly**

witness Shylock on the warpath – after the break

Act 3 *scene* 1

◆ Solanio and Salerio consider the rumor that Antonio's ship is wrecked.

◆ Shylock confirms his intention to have revenge if it is true.

◆ Shylock's friend, Tubal, brings news of Jessica and confirms the rumor of a shipwreck.

Shakespeare begins this act by bringing the audience's attention back to the bond between Shylock and Antonio. Solanio and Salerio have more information to suggest that Antonio has lost a ship. They seek further news from Shylock after teasing him cruelly about Jessica's elopement.

The three characters discuss the bond. Shylock makes it clear that he disapproves of lending money for a Christian courtesy, without charging interest, and restates his intention to avenge Antonio if the agreement is broken.

○ Look for the lines that give Shylock's point of view about the treatment he has suffered from Antonio.

Shylock says Antonio goads him for the simple reason that he is a Jew. He goes on to point out that Jews are no different from Christians as human beings. Because a sufferer of wrongs is likely to seek revenge if a Christian, he argues that Jews are no different and so would be justified in wanting revenge.

Solanio and Salerio are summoned by Antonio, and a new character, Tubal, is introduced. Tubal is a friend of Shylock's who brings news of Jessica spending his money wildly, and confirms Antonio's shipwreck. Shakespeare makes Tubal present the news about the ship when only Shylock is present. ○ Why do you think this is?

The entire scene is written in prose although the characters appearing in it usually speak in verse. This probably reflects confidentiality between Solanio and Salerio, and a relaxation of their usual formality because they are concerned about Antonio.

Shylock lets down his reserve because he is angry and upset about Jessica and the lost riches that she has taken with her. This further fuels his hatred of Christians. He speaks in repetitive exclamations as he becomes quite excited and glad that Antonio has run into trouble. Shakespeare mixes up these several complaints in the conversation with Tubal to emphasize Shylock's rage, and to show how Antonio is becoming his object of revenge – all Christians for all Jews.

By this stage in the play, the main threads of the plot have been developed. Just as the caskets plot has been peeled away to clear the way for Bassanio, so the hints and foreboding about the bond stated at earlier stages in the play are becoming serious grounds for concern. We know how strongly the characters feel about each other, how their beliefs make them act, how seriously they must undertake trials. The audience should now be thoroughly involved in the plot and have developed loyalties, hopes, and feelings about the characters. ○ How sympathetic do you feel toward Shylock at this point in the play?

Act 3 *scene* 2

◆ Bassanio chooses the lead casket and wins Portia.
◆ Gratiano and Nerissa announce their intention to marry.
◆ Lorenzo and Jessica arrive.
◆ Salerio delivers bad news to Bassanio from Antonio.
◆ The bond is explained to Portia and discussed.
◆ The rings plot is introduced.

In this long scene, all three pairs of lovers come together in the romantic atmosphere of Belmont. Bassanio makes the speech of a wise man when he chooses the lead casket. This confirms to the audience that he is a man of good character with fine qualities, who deserves Portia.

As they exchange sweet words, Portia gives Bassanio a love token – a ring, which she tells him he is not to part with under any circumstances.

Note that Portia says to Bassanio: … *confess/ What treason there is mingled with your love* (lines 27–28). Bassanio replies that the uncertainty surrounding the outcome of the test is the only factor affecting the full expression of his love, but the real confession seems to come later (lines 268–271) when he reveals to Portia:

you shall see/ How much I was a braggart. When I told you/ My state was nothing, I should then have told you/ That I was worse than nothing.

In an echo of the main pair of lovers, Gratiano seeks – and is given – permission to marry Nerissa. Lorenzo and Jessica arrive to complete the trio.

Salerio delivers a letter from Antonio to Bassanio discharging Bassanio from all debts and asking him to come to Venice before Antonio's death. ❍ What effect does the letter have on the appearance of its reader?

Portia is made fully aware of Bassanio's circumstances, and the bond is discussed. She suggests that many more times the original sum of the loan be repaid, but Jessica has warned that Shylock *would rather have Antonio's flesh/ Than twenty times the value of the sum.*

Shakespeare is entertaining the audience with romance and delays dealing with the main plot of the bond to increase suspense. Events in the lives of each pair of lovers have developed significantly and information about the relationships between them prepares the audience for events later in the play, particularly the courtroom scene.

Portia and Bassanio make their series of elegant speeches in strictly formal blank verse. Music plays as a symbol of love and harmony as Bassanio chooses. ✪ Find the words that rhyme with "lead" at the beginning of the song. These may be intended as a hint to help him.

Over to you

? What does Shylock tell Salerio he would use Antonio's flesh for?

? Who or what is Bassanio talking about when he says: *Thy paleness moves me more than eloquence*?

? Explain Portia's play on words in scene 2, line 326: *Since you are dear bought, I will love you dear.*

Act 3 *scene* 3

◆ Shylock is determined to have his bond.
◆ Antonio is resigned to his fate.

Shylock speaks the words *I'll have my bond* several times – almost as a chant – during this scene. This repetition reinforces his power and determination.

Despite what is happening to him, Antonio is clearheaded. In answer to Solanio's suggestion that the Duke *Will never grant this forfeiture to hold*, he reasons that justice and the law will be ridiculed if Shylock is cheated of what he is rightfully owed. ✪ What reason does Antonio give to Solanio for Shylock hating him so much?

Act 3 *scene* 4

♦ Portia leaves Belmont in Lorenzo's care, and pretends to go to a monastery with Nerissa until the two husbands return.
♦ Balthasar is sent to Portia's cousin, Doctor Bellario.
♦ Portia tells Nerissa they will go to Venice dressed as men.

 The scene opens with Lorenzo's confirmation of Antonio's worth. Portia has already extended friendship toward him despite not having met him. He is Bassanio's friend, and that is enough to secure her help. From this point in the play until the end, Portia is in control. From her instructions to Balthasar, we gather that Portia has a plan. ❖ What items does she expect her cousin to give to Balthasar, and what hints does Portia give you about the nature of the plan?

Portia explains to Nerissa that the husbands will soon see their wives but they will not recognize them through the male disguise. The two women prepare to leave for Venice, and the audience is left wondering what Portia has in mind.

Act 3 *scene* 5

♦ Jessica, Lancelet, and Lorenzo discuss her change of faith.

Jessica and Lancelet are apparently in midconversation at the start of this comic scene. It is the first time we learn that Jessica may feel worried about the effect of her actions on her soul. Lancelet teases her, saying that she will be damned for being Shylock's daughter. He adds that changes of faith push up the price of pork because Jews do not eat it and Christians do. The way in which he does this is probably meant to cheer her up.

Lancelet and Lorenzo discuss dinner, and Jessica praises Portia as if she were a saint (lines 72–82). ❖ How does Jessica's praise of Portia prepare the audience for the next scene?

 Witty plays on words are exchanged between Lancelet and Lorenzo. Most of these are connected with meat and preparations for dinner. Such images anticipate Shylock's preparation for taking Antonio's pound of flesh, in the next scene.

Now Try This

? At the start of scene 3, Shylock says: *Tell me not of mercy*. What is the significance of this remark at this stage in the play?

? Which of Portia's words in her speech at scene 4, line 69 tell you how old she intends to look and seem when disguised?

? How far does Portia hope to travel on the day she and Nerissa leave for Venice?

? Make two columns on a piece of paper, one for Venice and one for Belmont. Under each heading, write down what has happened there in the first three acts.

now take a break before Portia saves the day

Act 4 *scene* 1

◆ Characters in the courtroom try several arguments to persuade Shylock to take money and forget the bond.

◆ Shylock is adamant that he will have his bond.

◆ Portia, disguised as Balthasar, unsuccessfully argues the case for mercy.

◆ Portia successfully argues the case in law.

◆ Shylock loses the case and is shown little mercy.

◆ Antonio persuades Bassanio to give the ring to Portia.

This is the longest and most important scene in the play. It brings the main theme of justice versus mercy to a climax and demonstrates that nothing, even justice, is more important than human kindness and mercy. There are sound religious reasons for a Christian to believe this. As Portia puts it: *... in the course of justice none of us/ Should see salvation* (lines 205–206). The scene also deals with revenge and retribution as Shylock falls into his own trap and is undone.

Shylock will have his bond

In an echo of the very first scene, this one opens with a sense that Antonio is doomed. He demonstrates that he understands and is prepared to accept his fate. This attitude of stoical, patient resignation contrasts strongly with Shylock's *tyranny and rage*, further emphasizing the difference between them.

The Duke asks Shylock to be merciful, suggesting that Antonio has had such bad luck lately that even the most hard-hearted people would have sympathy for him (lines 17–35). An obstinate Shylock does not give the *gentle answer* that the Duke hopes for. He says he will have what is rightfully his because it is his whim, although he eventually gives more than enough reason when he says (lines 59–61): *So can I give no reason, nor will I not/ More than a lodged hate and a certain loathing/ I bear Antonio.*

Bassanio's assertion that such cruelty is not justified also fails to move Shylock. It is ironic that Shylock says: *I am not bound to please thee with my answers*, because not only is Bassanio bound to Shylock through Antonio, but it further demonstrates Shylock's firm position as one who only believes in binding agreements. He does not recognize qualities such as mercy.

After another attempt by Bassanio to reason with Shylock, Antonio tries to hasten the judgment so that he may die with dignity (lines 71–84). Ever hopeful, Bassanio offers double the money, and Shylock says that many times the original value would make no difference to his determination to have the bond.

Since all other attempts to move Shylock have failed, the Duke comes back to the subject of mercy as the only possible argument left. This also has the effect of preparing us for Portia's speech on mercy. Shylock continues not to recognize higher qualities than justice, saying he has earned his payment and wants it just as much as many citizens of Venice want the slaves they have paid for.

All arguments now exhausted, the Duke hopes for the arrival of the lawyer, Bellario. Bassanio hopes for a modification of the bond in which Bassanio's *flesh, bones, blood, and all*, may be substituted for Antonio's. Shakespeare engineers the plot so that the Duke's wish is immediately granted. He reads the letter delivered by Nerissa, who is dressed as a legal clerk.

Shylock sharpens the knife

Suspense mounts as we hope for some reprieve, and Shylock coldly and *earnestly* sharpens a knife: *To cut the forfeiture from that bankrupt there.*

In his desperation to help Antonio, Gratiano almost loses his temper with Shylock. He declares that he begins to believe an ancient Greek idea that the spirit of wild animals gets into people, implying that Shylock is behaving like an animal.

Portia argues for mercy

A clerk reads aloud Bellario's letter recommending the young lawyer, Balthasar, who is Portia in disguise. She is readily welcomed by the court, and proceeds in a confident businesslike manner despite the disguise. As if there is little difference between them, she asks: *Which is the merchant here? And which the Jew?* She highlights the issue at stake, and then makes her important speech on the quality of mercy (lines 190–212).

She explains the subtle nature of mercy and that it is a gift from God to be given freely rather than forced. It is a great good for both the giver and the receiver and shows great strength of character in the giver. She says mercy is one of God's qualities handed down to kings who believed they represented God directly. No one would be saved if we insisted on justice. Mercy is superior to all the earthly trappings of kings, and showing it is the nearest that humans can get to becoming gods themselves.

Even Portia's eloquence cannot move the vengeful Shylock, however. She rejects Bassanio's plea to change the course of justice and earns the respect of Shylock, who compares her to the biblical character David, a wise young judge.

Shylock will not budge

After several more brief attempts to persuade Shylock to soften, he says (lines 236–237): *An oath, an oath! I have an oath in heaven/ Shall I lay perjury upon my soul?* and (lines 250–251): *There is no power in the tongue of man/ To alter me. I stay here on my bond.* There is irony in both these statements. The oath echoes the earthly bond Shylock is being asked to dissolve on the grounds of higher principles. There is no higher authority than heaven from which the quality of mercy may be given if Shylock were to break his oath. There is irony in the second statement because although Portia is in disguise and her character would have been played by a male actor in Shakespeare's time, it is the tongue of a woman that will soon force Shylock to give up the bond.

All seems lost

By this point in the scene (lines 240–241), all seems lost. Portia seems to agree that Shylock may take Antonio's flesh, and Shakespeare makes sure that the blood is to be spilled in front of the audience in order to increase the tension to its maximum potential.

When Portia asks: *Are there balance here to weigh the flesh?* (line 267), we are reminded of the scales of justice. The direction of the trial also changes from this point in the scene. All attempts to persuade Shylock to give up the bond have failed. It is now time for good-byes, though the audience still hopes for some way out of the terrible predicament that Antonio is in.

Shylock is so determined to stick to the terms of the bond that he will not even pay for a surgeon to tend the wound Antonio is about to receive. Antonio makes a dignified farewell speech to a grieving Bassanio.

In contrast to the gravity of Antonio's speech (lines 276–293) and Bassanio's loving reply, the new wives make asides to comment on the statements made by their husbands, who say they would sacrifice their women to save Antonio. By doing this, Shakespeare is giving the audience some brief comic relief from the tension and seriousness of the scene so far, and reminding us that there is some business other than the lawsuit yet to be resolved.

Portia argues in law

Portia cleverly and coolly drops the bombshell on Shylock, after having given him every opportunity to relent (lines 318–325). If he spills one *jot of blood,* his land and possessions will be confiscated by the State. Ironically, it is strict enforcement of the law, which Shylock has been so insistent about, rather than higher considerations that wins the day.

In cruel echoes of his own earlier words, statements to the effect that the young lawyer is outstanding now come from Gratiano rather than from Shylock. The bloodthirsty villain realizes he has no choice but to abide by the best financial offer that has been made to him. But Portia mocks and taunts him and points out that: *The law hath yet another hold on you* (line 362).

Portia explains that if an alien (a foreigner) is found guilty of trying to kill a Venetian citizen, the guilty party loses half his assets to the injured citizen and half to the State. In a display of mercy and *the difference of our spirit,* the Duke spares Shylock's life and the indignity it would cost him to beg for it. Nonetheless, Shylock says he cannot live with all his means taken away from him.

In a further display of mercy, Antonio settles the terms of Shylock's release. Shylock is required to give half his assets to Antonio, to use and hold in trust for Jessica. When Shylock dies, all must go to Lorenzo and Jessica. Antonio adds that Shylock must become a Christian. Not surprisingly, this prospect leaves Shylock feeling ill, and he quietly leaves the stage for the last time in the play.

Bassanio gives away the ring

Following the Duke's request for the merchant to reward the clever young lawyer, Bassanio and Antonio offer Portia money for her services. She refuses but, on being pressed, asks for the ring she has given him as a marriage gift. Despite his protests, Bassanio, at the request of both Portia as Balthasar, and Antonio, gives up the ring. The audience knows this will create the *unquiet house* Nerissa has mentioned earlier (line 306).

Shakespeare achieves maximum dramatic impact from revealing the loophole in the law by concealing it from the audience as well as the other characters. He also makes sure we don't forget who the young lawyer and his clerk really are, in preparation for the final act.

The imagery of sheep preyed upon by bloodthirsty wolves is often used in this scene to illustrate the relationship between the helpless Antonio and the powerful Shylock (lines 74–75, 116–117, 135–136, 140). ❍ What other animals are referred to in this scene? Why do you think Shakespeare uses these animal pictures?

As Shylock sharpens the knife, and tension is mounting, Gratiano uses several words that create images of knives (lines 125–128). Look them up and write them down.

Act 4 *scene* 2

◆ Portia and Nerissa pursue Shylock to sign the deed.
◆ Nerissa tells Portia of her plan to get the ring from Gratiano that she had given him.

This short and simple scene ties up loose ends with Shylock. Now that the tense time has passed, any sense of flatness or anticlimax is prevented by introducing a simple and entertaining echo of the rings plot already established between the main pair of lovers.

Can you remember?

? What does Shylock sharpen the knife on and how do you know?

? Who says: *How much more elder art thou than thy looks*?

? What does Bassanio say to try to change the course of justice?

? Why do you think Portia takes so long to reveal the loophole in the law that will save Antonio?

? Divide a piece of paper into two columns. In one column list the main points that Shylock could use to appeal against the judgment. In the other column list the main points that support the judgment.

now take a break before the loose ends are tied up

Act 5 *scene* 1

- Lorenzo and Jessica whisper "sweet nothings" in the garden.
- The main characters return to Belmont.
- Portia is introduced to Antonio for the first time.
- The lovers quarrel over the rings.
- Antonio makes another bond on Bassanio's behalf to Portia.
- Antonio has news that three ships have returned safely.
- Jessica and Lorenzo learn of their inheritance.

The caretaker lovers Jessica and Lorenzo make romantic speeches to each other and tell stories of other famous lovers in a kind of game until the servant, Stephano, brings news that Portia is about to return from the monastery. Lancelet says Bassanio is also about to return from Venice with good news.

The pretty speeches continue and the topic of music that has been started by Jessica and Lorenzo is picked up by Portia and Nerissa. Portia instructs everyone at Belmont to keep her absence secret from Bassanio and Gratiano.

No sooner has Antonio been introduced to Portia than the squabbles about the rings begin. The audience is full of anticipation as Nerissa and Gratiano first rehearse their squabble. The significance of the rings mounts by this device to such an extent that Bassanio, worried about Portia's reaction to his loss, in an aside, thinks: *Why, I were best to cut my left hand off/ And swear I lost the ring defending it* (lines 190–191).

For the first time in the play, Bassanio is in a situation that involves an oath for which he must take continuing responsibility. He has to face it himself, not pass it on to a friend or undertake a test that someone else has devised. He has married Portia, but the new oath regarding the ring seems to be the point when they are truly wed and Bassanio has learned some lessons about how seriously vows and oaths must be taken. He seems at last to have matured.

Eventually, after much taunting from the women, all is well, the truth about the disguises in court is revealed, Antonio's ships are safe, and Lorenzo is given his good news about the riches he and Jessica can look forward to after Shylock's death. As bawdy comments close the play, all lovers are in harmony, and Antonio has to content himself with the good news about his ships.

The players return to the romance and harmony of Belmont for the closing scene of the play. Gardens are traditionally romantic settings referring to classical myths and tales of paradise. It is a fitting way to set the scene for the expression of romantic love that will take place between the three pairs of lovers reunited at Belmont.

Bassanio and Portia's entertaining exchanges about the ring gain much of their effect from the repetition of the word "ring" at the end of almost every line. This repetition has the effect of sounding like an echo, and it also reinforces the idea of something very trivial assuming great importance.

Again, music as a symbol of harmony prevails in the atmosphere of Belmont and there are many references to day and night. It is the end of one day and the start of another. Gone are the troubles of the last four acts – the lovers are about to embark on the new era of married life.

Now Try This

? In lines 116–117 Portia says: *How many things by season seasoned are/ To their right praise and true perfection!* What do you think she means?

? What does Antonio offer as a forfeit if Bassanio breaks the vow he makes in this scene?

? Some people think the play should end with the trial

scene, and that act 5 is unnecessary. Do you agree?

? What is the significance of music in this play?

? Look at the summary list of key points below. Try to put them in the right order (answers at bottom of page):

A Bassanio wins Portia.

B Shylock is punished.

C Portia saves Antonio.

D Shylock is angry, and Antonio is in trouble.

E Gratiano and Nerissa announce their intention to marry.

F All lovers are united at Belmont.

G Antonio enters into the bond with Shylock.

H Gobbo goes to work for Bassanio.

I Jessica and Lorenzo elope.

J The Princes of Morocco and Arragon choose the wrong caskets.

ANSWERS

1G Antonio enters into the bond with Shylock.

2H Gobbo goes to work for Bassanio.

3I Jessica and Lorenzo elope.

4J The Princes of Morocco and Arragon choose the wrong caskets.

5D Shylock is angry, and Antonio is in trouble.

6A Bassanio wins Portia.

7E Gratiano and Nerissa announce their intention to marry.

8C Portia saves Antonio.

9B Shylock is punished.

10F All lovers are united at Belmont.

Treat yourself to a break before you show off what you know

TOPICS FOR DISCUSSION AND BRAINSTORMING

Studying is easier and more fun if you vary your approach to it. Devise games, work with a friend, concentrate on your own, make lists, draw maps and pictures, write essay plans, and remember to reward yourself.

One of the best ways to review is with one or more friends. Even if you're with someone who hardly knows the text you're studying, you'll find that having to explain things to your friend will help you to organize your own thoughts and memorize key points. If you're with someone who has studied the text, you'll find that the things you can't remember are different from the things your friend can't remember, so you'll help each other.

Discussion will also help you to develop interesting new ideas that perhaps neither of you would have had alone. Use a **brainstorming** approach to tackle any of the topics listed below. Allow yourself to share whatever ideas come into your head, however meaningless they seem. This will get you thinking creatively.

Whether alone or with a friend, use Mind Mapping (see p. x) to help you brainstorm and organize your ideas. If you are with a friend, use a large sheet of paper and colored pens.

Any of the topics below could appear on an exam, but be sure to answer the precise question given.

Character

1　Write a résumé for a character in the play who might be applying for a job. Include age, interests, education, qualifications, and personal qualities.

2　Which of these characters are Antonio's friends? Check the ones you think are:
Bassanio/Solanio/Shylock/Gobbo/Gratiano/Salerio/Tubal/ Balthasar.

3　What do you think of Jessica's attitude toward her father?

4　Which characters speak in prose and why?

5 What is wrong with Portia's suitors who leave Belmont without taking the test? Make a list for each one. See act 1, scene 2 if you need to be reminded.
6 Who picks which casket?
7 Have you heard the expression "a wolf in sheep's clothing"? How appropriate a description is this of Shylock?

Language

1 Who said the following, and what do they mean? If you can't remember, look them up!

In sooth, I know not why I am so sad (act 1, scene 1).
I will feed fat the ancient grudge I bear him (act 1, scene 3).
O what a goodly outside falsehood hath (act 1, scene 3).
All things that are/ Are with more spirit chased than enjoyed (act 2, scene 6).
Hanging and wiving goes by destiny (act 2, scene 9).
For were he out of Venice I can make what merchandise I will (act 3, scene 1).
The world is still deceived with ornament (act 3, scene 2).
That in the course of justice none of us/ Should see salvation (act 4, scene 1).
To do a great right, do a little wrong (act 4, scene 1).

2 Add the next line to the following quotations:
Hath not a Jew (act 3, scene 1, line 58).
The quality of mercy is not strained (act 4, scene 1, line 190).

3 What is an iambic foot?
4 What are the characteristics of Shakespearean verse?
5 Some words have been left out of Portia's speech that outwits Shylock. If you can't remember the exact word, add one that means the same and maintains the iambic rhythm:

Tarry a little, there is something _____
This bond doth give _____ here no _____ of blood;
The _____ expressly are "a _____ of flesh."
Take then thy _____, take thou thy pound of _____,
But in the _____ it if thou dost shed
One drop of _____ blood, thy _____ and _____
Are by the _____ of Venice confiscate
Unto the _____ of Venice.

Structure

1 List the plots. What is their order of importance in your opinion?

2 The nine short scenes in act 2 bounce from Belmont to Venice, back to Belmont, then to Venice again, and back to Belmont. How would you deal with this if you were staging a production?

3 How is location used in the play?

4 Which part of the play do you find easiest to understand?

5 Which part is the most difficult? What can you do to improve your understanding?

6 What are the rules of the caskets test?

7 How believable do you find the caskets plot? Do you think Shakespeare gives us logical reasons for Portia's suitors choosing the caskets they do?

8 How convincing is the trial scene?

9 Some people think the play should end with the trial scene, and that act 5 is unnecessary. Do you agree?

Themes and Issues

1 If you were Antonio, would you enter into this kind of bond? How would you deal with the difficult situation he finds himself in as a result?

2 What do you think Shakespeare's own attitude to Jews was?

3 How far do you think attitudes toward black people and Jews have changed since Shakespeare's time?

4 Should justice be seasoned with mercy?

5 What do you think of Shylock being made to change his faith? Do you think the Christians would afterward treat him as an equal?

6 What do you think would have been fair treatment of Shylock at the trial?

In all your study, in coursework, and in exams, be aware of the following:

- **Characterization** – the characters and how we know about them (what they say and do, how the author describes them), their relationships, and how they develop.
- **Plot and structure** – what happens and how the plot is organized into parts or episodes.
- **Setting and atmosphere** – the changing scene and how it reflects the story (for example, a rugged landscape and a storm reflecting a character's emotional difficulties).
- **Style and language** – the author's choice of words, and literary devices such as imagery, and how these reflect the mood.
- **Viewpoint** – how the story is told (for example, through an imaginary narrator, or in the third person but through the eyes of one character – "She was furious – how dare he!").
- **Social and historical context** – influences on the author (see Background in this guide).

Develop your ability to:

- Relate **detail** to **broader content, meaning, and style**.
- Show understanding of the author's **intentions, technique, and meaning** (brief and appropriate comparisons with other works by the same author will earn credit).
- Give **personal response and interpretation**, backed up by **examples** and short **quotations**.
- **Evaluate** the author's achievement (how far does the author succeed and why?)

THE EXAM ESSAY

PLANNING

Writing an excellent essay on a theme from *The Merchant of Venice* will challenge your essay writing skills, so it is important to spend some time carefully planning your essay.

1 **Mind Map** your ideas, without worrying about their order yet.
2 **Order** the relevant ideas (the ones that really relate to the question) by numbering them in the order in which you will write the essay.
3 **Gather** your evidence and short quotes.

You could remember this as the **MOG** technique.

WRITING AND CHECKING

Then write the essay, allowing five minutes at the end for checking relevance, and spelling, grammar, and punctuation.

REMEMBER!

Stick to the question, and always **back up** your points with evidence in the form of examples and short quotations. Note: You can use ". . ." for unimportant words left out of a quotation.

MODEL ANSWER AND ESSAY PLAN

The next (and final) chapter consists of a model answer to an exam question on *The Merchant of Venice*, followed by essay plans. Don't be discouraged if you think you couldn't write an essay as good as this one yet. This is a top "A"-grade essay, a standard at which to aim. You'll develop your skills if you work at them. Even if you're reading this the night before the exam, you can easily memorize the MOG technique in order to do your personal best.

The model answer and essay plans are good examples for you to follow, but don't try to learn them by heart. It's better to pay close attention to the wording of the question you choose to answer on the exam, and allow Mind Mapping to help you to think creatively.

M ODEL ANSWER AND ESSAY PLANS

QUESTION

Riches and wealth can be seen to be of two kinds: the possession of money and material things, or spiritual riches such as love and generosity. In *The Merchant of Venice*, Shakespeare explores and contrasts both kinds of wealth.

PLAN

1 Strong opening paragraph giving thesis, setting, title, and author of literary work considered.
2 Contrast in character between Antonio and Shylock, and others' opinions of both characters.
3 Discussion of Portia and the significance of the caskets.
4 The trial scene.
5 Significance of contrast between Venice and Belmont.
6 Strong conclusion, echoing the thesis of the essay: Spiritual riches are more valuable than material wealth.

ESSAY

Shakespeare's play *The Merchant of Venice*, set in Venice and the imaginary country house called Belmont in the Italian countryside, explores the importance of both material and spiritual wealth. Venice, where the play opens, was an extremely rich city on the Adriatic whose wealth was due to the fact that it was on the trade route to the East.

Antonio, the prosperous merchant of Venice of the play's title, is presented as an ideal friend and Christian whose generosity is well known and who happily offers his friend, Bassanio, a large loan at no interest. Solanio, another friend of Antonio's, says, "A kinder man treads not the earth." In contrast to Antonio, Shylock, the Jewish moneylender, is presented as miserly and greedy, an "inhuman wretch," who, because of his religion, has no qualms about charging a high interest on the loans he makes. It is suggested that when his

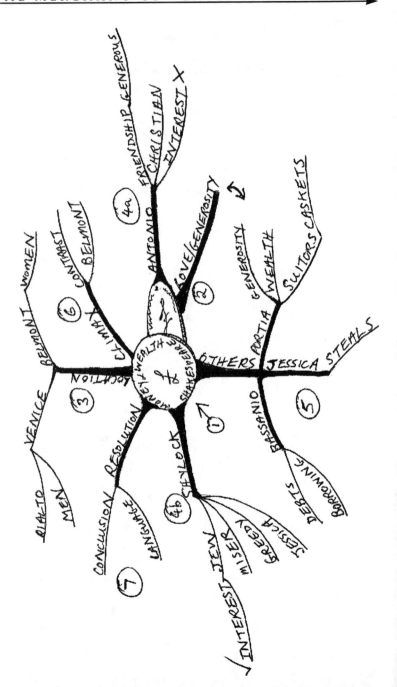

daughter, Jessica, runs away from him, he is more upset about the loss of the money she takes with her than her own departure. Money is of supreme importance to Shylock, more important than family affection or mercy.

In Belmont, outside of Venice, Portia, a young heiress, has been left three caskets—of gold, silver, and lead—by her dead father, and is to marry the suitor who guesses correctly which one contains her portrait. The lesson of the caskets is that you should not discriminate against the modest, for "All that glisters is not gold."

In the play's main climax, the trial scene, Shylock demands his pound of flesh, suggesting that he seeks revenge rather than justice, and it is the unselfish Portia, whose generosity can be compared with Antonio's, who is the agent of Shylock's humiliation. Shylock is forced to give up both his money and his religion and loses both of those things that are of the greatest importance to him.

Shakespeare uses the two settings to symbolize the differing qualities of love and material wealth. Venice is presented as a place of commerce where money is all-important, and Belmont, Portia's home, is presented as a place far from the tensions of business negotiations. The ending of the play concludes the victory of love and pleasure over money and business. The characters (except Shylock) unite in Belmont and let its peace and beauty soothe the damage that greed and money have caused.

In conclusion, Shakespeare seems to be suggesting that true wealth and prosperity of mind and spirit come from giving rather than receiving, and that the love and friendship you gain from your relationships with others will grant you more satisfaction than social status or financial success. Shylock, who symbolizes the love of money, is punished at the end of the play, while Portia, Bassanio, and Antonio are rewarded with life, love, and hope for the future.

WHAT'S SO GOOD ABOUT IT?

1 Opens with a strong thesis statement.
2 Awareness of audience/reader.

3 Suitable use of short quotations from the text.

4 Understanding of characters in the play.

5 Awareness of historical context of the play.

6 Discusses the importance of setting in the play.

7 Shows clear understanding of the play's plot.

8 Logical and persuasive argument.

9 Uses vivid and lively vocabulary.

10 Obeys the conventions of standard written English.

11 Is well organized.

12 Concludes with a strong summary of thesis statement.

Here are some more question essay plans

QUESTION

For part of the 1700s, *The Merchant of Venice* was known as *The Jew of Venice*. Which is the more suitable title and why?

PLAN

- Intro – brief explanation of why this was.
- Why Antonio is central to the play.
- Why Shylock is central to the play (speeches).
- Relationship between them/ similarities and differences between them.
- How Shakespeare uses them to develop themes.
- Significance of Venice to trade and to audience.
- Conclusion – who I think the key character is, and which is best title.

QUESTION

How important are race and religion in *The Merchant of Venice*?

PLAN

- Intro – Jewishness very important, drives main plot.
- Explain concept of racism – Elizabethan/modern attitudes.
- Relevance of Shylock and Morocco.
- Shylock, Jessica, and Jews.

- Morocco, slaves (reflects Elizabethan England)/Portia – imagery.
- Conclusion (relevance to other themes).

FURTHER QUESTIONS

Here are some more essay questions of the type you can expect to see on an exam. Try writing a Mind Map for each one, then compare notes with a friend who has done the same.

1 Discuss the view that Shylock is as much sinned against as sinning.
2 *All that glisters is not gold.* Through detailed reference to the text, show how Shakespeare treats the theme of appearance and reality.
3 Choose a speech from the play and give reasons why you consider it to be important. Take special note of language and how it develops themes, character, and the course of events.

GLOSSARY OF LITERARY TERMS

alliteration   repetition of a sound at the beginnings of words; for example, *daughter, ducats.*

aside   a short speech spoken by one character, as if thinking aloud, not meant to be heard by others on stage.

blank verse   the kind of nonrhyming verse, with five pairs of syllables to each line, in which Shakespeare usually writes. Also called **iambic pentameter**.

comedy   in Shakespeare, those plays that feature at least some humor, and have happy endings (usually marriages) and no deaths.

context   the social and historical influences on the author.

couplet   *see* rhyming couplet.

dramatic irony   *see* irony (dramatic).

foreshadowing   an indirect warning of things to come, often through imagery.

iambus   an iambic foot of two syllables.

iambic feet   *see* blank verse.

image   a word picture used to make an idea come alive; for example, a **metaphor, simile,** or **personification** (*see* separate entries).

imagery   the kind of word picture used to make an idea come alive.

irony   (**dramatic**) where at least one character on stage is unaware of an important fact that the audience knows about, and that is somehow hinted at; (**simple**) where a character says the opposite of what he or she really thinks, or pretends to be ignorant of the true facts, usually to show scorn or ridicule.

metaphor   a description of a thing as if it were something essentially different but also in some way similar; for example, in act 1, scene 1, Gratiano tells Antonio *But fish not with this melancholy bait/ For this fool gudgeon, this opinion*; he means that good opinion is like a fish to be caught.

personification   a description of something abstract as if it were a person; for example, ... *the sweet wind did gently kiss the trees* (act 5, scene 1).

prose   language in which, unlike verse, there is no set number of syllables in a line, and no rhyming.

pun   a use of a word with two meanings, or of two similar-sounding words, where both meanings are appropriate in different ways.

rhyming couplet   a pair of rhyming lines, often used at the end of a speech.

setting   the place in which the action occurs, usually affecting the atmosphere; in *The Merchant of Venice* this is always either Belmont or Venice.

simile   a comparison of two things that are different in most ways but similar in one important way; for example, *His reasons are as two grains of wheat hid in two bushels of chaff* (Bassanio, act 1, scene 1).

structure   how the plot is organized.

theme   an idea explored by an author; for example, money and wealth.

viewpoint   how the story is told; for example, through action, or in discussion between minor characters.

INDEX

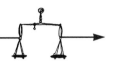

Page references in bold denote major character or theme sections